Praise for *The Body Is Not an Apology*

"From the moment I met Sonya Renee, I knew my life, my world, and the way I view myself and others around me would never be the same. *The Body Is Not an Apology* is essential reading for those of us who crave understanding and those who are already on the path to learning how beautiful and complex our bodies are. It will empower you with the tools to navigate a world that is often unkind to those of us who whether by choice or design don't adhere to society's standard of beauty. Her words will echo in your heart, soul, and body just as they have in mine."

—**Tess Holliday, plus model, author, and founder of Eff Your Beauty Standards**

"*The Body Is Not an Apology* is a gift, a blessing, a prayer, a reminder, a sacred text. In it, Taylor invites us to live in a world where different bodies are seen, affirmed, celebrated, and just. Taylor invites us to break up with shame, to deepen our literacy, and to liberate our practice of celebrating every body and never apologizing for this body that is mine and takes care of me so well. This book cracked me open in ways that I'm so grateful for. I know it will do the same for you."

—**Alicia Garza, cocreator of the Black Lives Matter Global Network and Strategy + Partnerships Director, National Domestic Workers Alliance**

"*The Body Is Not an Apology* is a radical, merciful, transformational book that will give you deep insights, inspiration, and concrete tools for launching the revolution right inside your own beloved body. Written from deep experience, with a force of catalytic energy and so much love."

—**Eve Ensler, author of *The Vagina Monologues* and *In the Body of the World***

"In 2017, #thefirsttimeisawmyself was a trending hashtag and Netflix campaign. As a disabled woman, #thefirsttimeireadmyself may well have been this book. Thank you, Sonya. Bought two copies, one for me and one for my daughter."

—**Rebecca Cokely, Senior Fellow for Disability Policy, Center for American Progress, disability rights activist, and mom**

T0007072

"Sonya Renee Taylor is a treasure that this world simply does not deserve. *The Body Is Not an Apology* is the gift of radical love the world needs! We are all better off because of her presence, talent, compassion, and authentic work. Thank you, Sonya, for all that you do."

—**Jes Baker, aka The Militant Baker, author of** *Things No One Will Tell Fat Girls*

"In these times, when the search for answers to the mounting injustices in our world seems to confound us, Sonya Renee Taylor offers a simple but powerful place to begin: recovering our relationship with our own bodies. To build a world that works for everyone, we must first make the radical decision to love every facet of ourselves. Through lucid and courageous self-revelation, Taylor shows us how to realize the revolutionary potential of self-love. 'The body is not an apology' is the mantra we should all embrace."

—**Kimberlé Crenshaw, legal scholar and founder and Executive Director, African American Policy Forum**

The Body Is Not an Apology

The Body
Is Not an
Apology

The Power of Radical Self-Love

Second Edition

Sonya Renee Taylor

BK

Berrett–Koehler Publishers, Inc.

Berrett-Koehler Publishers, Inc.
1333 Broadway, Suite 1000
Oakland, CA 94612-1921
Tel: (510) 817-2277   Fax: (510) 817-2278   www.bkconnection.com

Ordering Information
Quantity sales. Special discounts are available on quantity purchases by corporations, associations, and others. For details, contact the "Special Sales Department" at the Berrett-Koehler address above.
Individual sales. Berrett-Koehler publications are available through most bookstores. They can also be ordered directly from Berrett-Koehler: Tel: (800) 929-2929; Fax: (802) 864-7626; www.bkconnection.com.
Orders for college textbook / course adoption use. Please contact Berrett-Koehler: Tel: (800) 929-2929; Fax: (802) 864-7626.

Distributed to the U.S. trade and internationally by Penguin Random House Publisher Services.

Berrett-Koehler and the BK logo are registered trademarks of Berrett-Koehler Publishers, Inc.

Printed in the United States of America

Berrett-Koehler books are printed on long-lasting acid-free paper. When it is available, we choose paper that has been manufactured by environmentally responsible processes. These may include using trees grown in sustainable forests, incorporating recycled paper, minimizing chlorine in bleaching, or recycling the energy produced at the paper mill.

Library of Congress Cataloging-in-Publication Data

Names: Taylor, Sonya Renee, author.
Title: The body is not an apology : the power of radical self-love / Sonya Renee Taylor.
Description: Second edition. | Oakland, CA : Berrett-Koehler Publishers, Inc., [2020] | Includes bibliographical references and index.
Identifiers: LCCN 2020040634| ISBN 9781523090990 (paperback) | ISBN 9781523091003 (adobe pdf) | ISBN 9781523091010 (epub)
Subjects: LCSH: Self-acceptance. | Self-perception. | Body image. | Human body.
Classification: LCC BF575.S37 T39 2021 | DDC 158.1—dc23
LC record available at https://lccn.loc.gov/2020040634

Second Edition
28 27 26 25 24 23   10 9 8 7 6

Set in Arno Pro by Westchester Publishing Services
Cover designer: Irene Morris, Morris Design

For Terry Lyn Hines (1959–2012)

My first and most enduring example
of the power of radical love.

My Mother's Belly

The bread of her waist, a loaf
I would knead with eight-year-old palms
sweaty from play. My brother and I marveled
at the ridges and grooves. How they would summit at her navel.
How her belly looked like a walnut. How we were once seeds
that resided inside. We giggled, my brother and I,
when she would recline on the couch,
lift her shirt, let her belly spread like cake batter in a pan.
It was as much a treat as licking the sweet from electric mixers on birthdays.

The undulating of my mother's belly was not
a shame she hid from her children.
She knew we came from this. Her belly was a gift
we kept passing between us.
It was both hers, of her body,
and ours for having made it new,
different. Her belly was an altar of flesh
built in remembrance of us, by us.

What remains of my mother's belly
resides in a container of ashes I keep in a closet.
Every once and again, I open the box,
sift through the fine crystals with palms
that were once eight. Feel the grooves and ridges
that do not summit now but rill through fingers.
Granules so much more salt
than sweet today. And yet, still I marvel
at her once body. Even in this form say,
"I came from this."

Contents

Foreword

I was eleven the first time I heard someone voice concern over the size and shape of my body. One of my aunts had come to visit with my mother one evening for wine and conversation. My brother and I were supposed to be asleep, but I couldn't pass up on the opportunity to hear what the adults talked about when the kids weren't around. It was exciting at first, hearing about their grown-up lives, their spats with coworkers and partners. They would laugh heartily and swear with abandon. Then I heard my aunt say to my mom, "You know, you need to be careful with her. She's not chubby-cute anymore; she's getting fat."

My mother paused for a minute and said with a sigh, "I'm not sure what to do about it."

I felt ice fill my veins as I crept out of my room to take a look at them. There they were, staring at my school picture proudly displayed on the wall.

The concern that my mother and my aunt had for the size and shape of my body was the same concern that their mothers had for them when they were girls. It was born from the fear that the world would be cruel to me if my body was not an acceptable size or shape, as the world had been cruel to them. They could not imagine a world that would love any woman in a larger body, and they wanted me to be loved. Their concern came from love, and that love felt like a knife to the heart.

As a Black girl, I quickly learned from others that there were many things about myself that needed to shrink. Not just my body—my laugh, my ambitions, my imagination, my will, and eventually my anger—everything I was would need to be less.

But even as I fought to make myself smaller, my self would fight back. The diets would not stick, the laughter would not quiet, the opinions would not hide, the anger would not die. Every attempt I made to be less of myself would fail, and I would come back bigger than ever—in every way.

It was not until I was in my thirties that it occurred to me that perhaps I didn't want to spend the rest of my life fighting myself. Perhaps the victory that lay at the end of the long road of self-denial and repression was not a reward that I actually wanted. Perhaps all the love and acceptance that had been promised me if I could just hate myself into a new me didn't exist. Perhaps I was going to spend my entire life fighting my own existence and then just . . . die.

I would like to say that this revelation led me to immediately toss a lifetime of self-loathing aside and fully embrace proud ownership of my self, but there are no epiphanies that outweigh a lifetime of conditioning. Slowly, and often painfully, I started to risk moments of authenticity. I started to share my opinion without apology. I started laughing loudly without embarrassment. I started creating and growing into myself. And slowly I started to believe that perhaps I did have the right to take up space. Perhaps I had not only the right but the obligation to love myself as I was.

I don't know who I would be if I hadn't decided that I didn't want to die fighting with myself. But I do know that I likely would not have met Sonya. I first met Sonya a few years after I had decided to take a giant leap of faith and trust that not only did my voice need to be heard but that my talents in writing and speaking were strong enough to warrant quitting my job and becoming a full-time writer. It was a gamble that more than paid off.

I also worked to love my physical body as I had been learning to love my brain, but that was the tougher battle. Most days, I felt fine. Moments of body shame would hit me a few times a day and I would quickly push them away, reminding myself that body shame was a tool of White supremacist, capitalist patriarchy.

But as my writing career took off and I found myself suddenly praised for the opinions that had always been deemed "too strong" and the tone that had always been called "too aggressive," I found myself increasingly battling voices that told me, "Okay, you can be loud, you can be opinionated, but you can't also be fat." With each new picture of myself I encountered in articles or after events, I would hear a voice that said, "Who do you think you are to be all the things we told you not to be? Black, angry, loud, and fat? What makes you so special that you think that not only do we have to listen to you, we have to look at you as well?"

I distinctly remember feeling very uncomfortable in my body when I was asked to share a stage with Sonya and a few other speakers at an event discussing race and gender. I remember having spent a few long minutes staring in the mirror backstage and lamenting that I hadn't found a way—while I was busy writing, speaking, and raising two kids—to also make my body a little smaller. I remember, as I was speaking onstage, regularly tugging at my dress that I was now convinced was highlighting my every physical flaw.

Then Sonya got onstage. She glided strongly and confidently across the floor in a beautiful dress, gorgeous hoop earrings, and one of the most welcoming smiles I had ever seen. She recited poetry that brought me home to my body, grounded me in it, and let me feel its strength. I listened to her speak and watched her move with awe. I was watching someone living—truly living—in their body. And I wanted that, even if just for a moment. I bought her book.

I am not the only person changed by this book or by Sonya Renee Taylor's work. Over the years I have heard from many friends and peers of all ages, races, and genders about what this book has meant to them on their journey to self-love. I have heard from many how this book has brought them back from the abyss of commercialized self-loathing and back into the truth of their own majesty.

Sonya envisions radical healing divorced from the ableist, capitalist White supremacy of traditional "self-help." She envisions healing not only for the self but for our communities. As the years go by, I find that her work is more vital than ever. As Sonya is ever growing and changing, as we all are, I'm glad to see this work, already a classic, grow and change as well. I hope that in these pages you find your moment of living, truly living, in your body and mind. I hope that moment leads to a lifetime of living in self-love. We all deserve to live our lives as our full selves, in all of our true beauty. I hope that you take a leap of faith in your own divinity and dive into the pages of this book with gusto. You will surely be rewarded.

Ijeoma Oluo

Prologue

Long before there was a digital media and education company or a radical self-love movement with hundreds of thousands of followers on our website and social media pages, before anyone cared to write about us in newsprint or interview me on television, before people began to send me photos of their bodies with my words etched in ink on their backs, forearms, and shoulders (which never stops being awesome and weird), there was a word . . . well, words. Those words were "your body is not an apology." It was the summer of 2010, in a hotel room in Knoxville, Tennessee. My team and I were preparing for evening bouts in competition at the Southern Fried Poetry Slam. Slam is competitive performance poetry. Teams and individuals get three minutes onstage to share what is often deeply intimate, personal, and political poetry, at which point five randomly selected judges from the audience score their poems on a scale from 0.0 to 10.0. It's a raucous game that takes the high art of poetry and brings it to the masses in bars, clubs, coffee shops, and National Poetry Slam Championship Tournaments around the country. Poetry slam is as ridiculous as it is beautiful; it is everything gauche and glorious about the power of the word. The slam is a place where the misfit and the marginalized (and the self-absorbed) have center stage and the rapt ears of an audience, if only for three minutes.

It was on a hotel bed in this city, preparing for this odd game, that I uttered the words "your body is not an apology" for the first time. My team was a kaleidoscope of bodies and identities. We were a microcosm of a world I would like to live in. We were Black, White, Southeast Asian. We are able-bodied and disabled. We were gay, straight, bi, and queer. What we brought to Knoxville that year were the stories of living in our bodies in all their complex tapestries. We were complicated and honest with each other, and this is how I wound up in a conversation with my teammate Natasha, an early-thirtysomething living with cerebral palsy and fearful she might be pregnant. Natasha told me how her potential pregnancy was most assuredly by a guy who was just an occasional fling. All of life was up in the air for Natasha, but she was abundantly clear that she had no desire to have a baby and not by this person. One of my many career iterations of the past was as a sexual-health and public-health service provider. This background made me notorious for asking people about their safer-sex practices, handing out condoms, and offering sexual-health harm-reduction strategies. Instinctually, I asked Natasha why she had chosen not to use a condom with this casual sexual partner with whom she had no interest in procreating. Neither Natasha nor I knew that my honest question and her honest answer would be the catalyst for a movement. Natasha told me her truth: "My disability makes sex hard already, with positioning and stuff. I just didn't feel like it was okay to make a big deal about using condoms."

When we hear someone's truth and it strikes some deep part of our humanity, our own hidden shames, it can be easy to recoil into silence. We struggle to hold the truths of others because we have so rarely had the experience of having our own truths held. Social researcher and expert on vulnerability and shame Brené Brown says, "If we can share our story with someone who responds with empathy and understanding, shame can't survive."[1] I understood the truth Natasha was sharing. Her words pricked some painful underbelly of knowing in my own body. My entire being rang in resonance. I was transported to all the times I had given away my own body in penance. A reel of memories scrolled through my mind of all the ways I told the world I was sorry for having this wrong, bad body. It was from this deep cave of mutual vulnerability that the words spilled from me: "Natasha, your body is not an apology. It is not something you give to someone to say, 'Sorry for my disability.'" She began to weep, and for a few minutes I just held my maybe-pregnant friend as she contemplated the fullness of what those words meant for her life and her body. There are times when our unflinching honesty, vulnerability, and empathy will create a transformative portal, an opening to a completely new way of living. Such a portal was created between Natasha and me that summer evening in Tennessee, because as the words escaped my lips some part of them remained stuck inside me. The words I said to Natasha in that hotel room were as much for me as they were for her. I was also telling myself, "Sonya, your body is not an apology."

At every turn, for days after my conversation with Natasha, the words returned to me like some sort of cosmic boomerang. They kept echoing off the walls of all my hidden hurts. Every time I uttered a disparaging word about my dimpled thighs I'd hear, "Your body is not an apology, Sonya." Each time I marked some erroneous statement with "My bad. I'm so stupid," my own inner voice would retort, "Your body is not an apology." Whenever my critical eye focused laser-like on some perceived imperfection of my own or some other human's being, the words would arrive like a well-trained butler to remind me, "Hey, the body is not an apology." My poet self knew that the words were demanding to be more than a passing conversation with a friend. They wanted more than my own self-flagellation. The words always had their own plans. Me, I was just a vessel.

A couple of years ago, I was listening to famed author and spiritual teacher Marianne Williamson share a talk on relationships. In it, she described the principle of natural intelligence. She posited, "An acorn does not have to say, 'I intend to become an oak tree.' Natural intelligence intends that every living thing become the highest form of itself and designs us accordingly."[2] In a single sentence, all in me that felt nameless was named. We have a dictionary full of terms describing our interpretation of natural intelligence. We sometimes call it purpose, other times, destiny. Although I agree with the spirit of those terms, I believe they fail to encapsulate the fullness of what Marianne Williamson's acorn example illustrates. Both *purpose* and *destiny* allude to a place we might, with enough effort, someday arrive. We belabor ourselves with all the things we must do to fulfill our purpose or live out our destiny. Contrary to purpose, natural intelligence does not require we do anything to achieve it. Natural intelligence imbues us with all we need at this exact moment to manifest the highest form of ourselves, and we don't have to figure out how to get it. We arrived on this planet with this source material already present. I am by no means implying that the work you may have done up to this point has been useless. To the contrary, I applaud whatever labor you have undertaken that has gotten you this far. Survival is damn hard. Each of us has traversed a gauntlet of traumas, shames, and fears to be where we are today, wherever that is. Each day we wake to a planet full of social, political, and economic obstructions that siphon our energy and diminish our sense of self. Consequently, tapping into this natural intelligence often feels nearly impossible. Humans unfortunately make being human exceptionally hard for each other, but I assure you, the work we have done or will do is not about acquiring some way of being that we currently lack. The work is to crumble the barriers of injustice and shame leveled against us so that we might access what we have always been, because we will, if unobstructed, inevitably grow into the purpose for which we were created: our own unique version of that oak tree.

Marianne Williamson offers us a perspective of natural intelligence as a source of innate perfect design, and yet her own bias and learned body shame contradict its efficacy. In her book *A Course in Weight Loss*, she conflates weight and healing, offering a world view that proposes weight loss as evidence of spiritual healing and alignment and weight gain as evidence of the contrary. Williamson fails to see the full forest of human weight diversity as the planet's quite clear proof of natural intelligence. With all her insight, even she is unable to see how her indoctrinated ideas about weight and size have demanded fat bodies apologize by pathologizing them and demanding they shrink. No matter how "enlightened" our ideas, none of us is immune to the social, political, and cultural indoctrinations of body shame. Without an intentional exploration of how (not if) we have adopted biased body-shame beliefs and a commitment to interrupting them as we continually seek to uncover them in ourselves, we will continue to obstruct the full manifestation of someone else's oak tree.

I have my own name for natural intelligence. I call it *radical self-love*, and this second edition is our opportunity to expand and unleash the full power of radical self-love as a tool for social change. In a time of unrest, uprisings, and a longing for what is possible beyond disconnection, radical self-love is a pathway toward personal and collective transformation. It is time we use it to change the world. Radical self-love was the force that cannoned the words "your body is not an apology" out of my mouth, directed toward a friend but ultimately barreling into my own chest and then into the hearts of hundreds of thousands of people around the world. Evangelizing radical self-love as the transformative foundation of how we make peace with our bodies, make peace with the bodies of others, and ultimately change the world is my highest calling. Coincidence after seeming coincidence has made that much evident. I don't know what your highest calling is. It's possible you don't quite know either. That is perfect. At this very second, a trembling acorn is plummeting from a branch, clueless as to why. It doesn't need to know why to fulfill its calling; it just needs us to get out of its way. Radical self-love is an engine inside you driving you to make your calling manifest. It is the exhaustion you feel every time the whispers of self-loathing, body shame, and doubt skulk through your brain. It is the contrary impulse that made you open this book, an action driven by a force so much larger than the voice of doubt and yet sometimes so much more difficult to hear.

Radical self-love is not a destination you are trying to get to; it is who you already are, and it is already working tirelessly to guide your life. The question is: How can you listen to it more distinctly, more often, even over the blaring of constant body shame? How can you allow it to change your relationship with your body and your world? And how can that change ripple throughout the entire planet? At the organization I founded, The Body Is Not an Apology, we are not saying anything new (see www.TheBodyIsNotAnApology.com). We are, however, connecting some straggling dots we believe others may have missed along the way. We know that the answer has always been love. The question is how do we stop forgetting the answer so we can get on with living our highest, most radically unapologetic lives. This book is my most sincere effort to help us all answer that.

The Body Is Not an Apology

1

Making Self-Love Radical

What Radical Self-Love Is and What It Ain't

Let me answer a couple of questions right away before you dig too deeply into this book and are left feeling bamboozled and hoodwinked. First, "Will this book fix my self-esteem, Sonya?" Nope. Second, "Will this book teach me how to have self-confidence?" Nah. Impromptu third question, "Well, then, why in Hades am I reading this book?" You are reading this book because your heart is calling you toward something exponentially more magnanimous and more succulent than self-esteem or self-confidence. You are being called toward radical self-love. While not completely unrelated to self-esteem or self-confidence, radical self-love is its own entity, a lush and verdant island offering safe harbor for self-esteem and self-confidence. Unfortunately, those two ships often choose to wander aimlessly adrift at sea, relying on willpower or ego to drive them, and in the absence of those motors are left hopelessly pursuing the fraught mirage of someday. As in, "Someday I will feel good enough about myself to shop that screenplay I wrote." Or, "Someday, when I

1

have self-confidence, I will get out of this raggedy relationship." Self-esteem and self-confidence are fleeting, and both can exist without radical self-love, but it almost never bodes well for anyone involved when they do. Think of all the obnoxious people you know oozing arrogance, folks we can be certain think extremely highly of themselves. Although you may call them . . . ahem . . . confident (at least that may be one of the things you call them), I bet the phrase *radical self-love* doesn't quite fit. Pick your favorite totalitarian dictator and you will likely find someone who has done just fine in the self-confidence category. After all, you would have to think you're the bee's knees to entertain the idea of single-handedly dominating the entire planet. The forty-fifth U.S. president strikes me as a man with epic self-confidence. "The Donald" is not struggling with his sense of self (even if the rest of the world is struggling with its sense of who he is). Even if we were to surmise that Trump and others like him are acting from an exaggerated lack of self-esteem or confidence, I think we can agree not many of their attitudes or actions feel like love.

The biggest flaw of investing our time in self-esteem and self-confidence is that neither model unto itself has the ability to reorient our world toward justice and compassion. Self-esteem and self-confidence aren't scalable. The term *scalable* is most frequently heard in the economic or business start-up world and is used to describe "a company's ability to grow without being hampered by its structure or available resources when faced with increased production."[1] If self-esteem and confidence are primarily fueled by ego and external conditions, they are inevitably going to be a shaky platform upon which to build full, abundant lives. If they can barely hold up our expanding dreams and awakenings, they are certain to buckle under the weight of oppression. On the contrary, radical self-love builds a foundation strong enough to carry the enormous power of our highest calling while also connecting us to the potential power of all bodies. If radical self-love is an oak tree, it is an essential part of an entire ecosystem. When it grows stronger, the entire system does as well. Radical self-love starts with the individual, expands to the family, community, and organization, and ultimately transforms society. All while still unwaveringly holding you in the center of that expansion. That, my friend, is scale.

You may be asking, "Okay, well, if this book won't help me with my self-esteem or self-confidence, will it at least teach me self-acceptance?" My short answer is, if I do my job correctly, no! Not because self-acceptance isn't useful, but because I believe there is a port far beyond the isle of self-acceptance and I want us to go there. Think back to all the times you "accepted" something and found it completely uninspiring. When I was a kid, my mother would make my brother and me frozen pot pies for dinner. It was the meal for the days she did not feel like cooking. I enjoyed the flaky pastry crust. The chunks of mechanically pressed chicken in a Band-Aid-colored beige gravy were tolerable. But there was nothing less appetizing than the abhorrent vegetable medley of peas, green beans, and carrots portioned throughout each bite like miserable stars in an endless galaxy. Yes, I ate those hateful mixed vegetables. Hunger will make you accept things. I accepted that my options were limited: pick out a million tiny peas or get a job at the ripe age of ten and figure out how to feed myself. Why am I talking about pot pies? Because self-acceptance is the mixed-veggie pot pie of radical self-love. It will keep you alive when the options are sparse, but what if there is a life beyond frozen pot pies?

Too often, *self-acceptance* is used as a synonym for *acquiescence.* We accept the things we cannot change. We accept death because we have no say over its arbitrary and indifferent arrival at our door. We have personal histories of bland acceptance. We have accepted lackluster jobs because we were broke. We have accepted lousy partners because their lousy presence was better than the hollow aloneness of their absence. We practice self-acceptance when we have grown tired of self-hatred but can't conceive of anything beyond a paltry tolerance of ourselves. What a thin coat to wear on this weather-tossed road. Famed activist and profes-

sor Angela Davis said, "I am no longer accepting the things I cannot
change. I am changing the things
I cannot accept."[2] We can change
the circumstances that have had us
settle for self-acceptance. I assure
you there is a richer, thicker, cozier
blanket to carry through the world.
There is a realm infinitely more
mind-blowing. It's called radical
self-love.

> **Radical Reflection**
> *Concepts like self-acceptance and body neutrality are not without value. When you have spent your entire life at war with your body, these models offer a truce. But you can have more than a cease-fire. You can have radical self-love because you are already radical self-love.*

Why the Body?

Humans are a varied and divergent bunch, with all manner of beliefs, morals, values, and ideas. We have struggled to find agreement on much of anything over the centuries (just think about how long we argued about gravity and whether the world is shaped like a pizza), but here is a completely noncontroversial statement I think we have consensus around: You, my dear, have a body. And should you desire to remain on this spinning rock hurtling through space, you will need a body to do it. Everything else we think we know is up for debate. Are we spiritual beings? Depends on whom you ask. Do humans have souls? Been fighting about that since Aristotle likened the souls of fetuses to those of vegetables.[3] But bodies—yup, we got those. And given this widely agreed-upon reality, it seems to me if ever there were a place where the practice of radical love could be a transformative force, the body ought to be that location.

When we speak of the ills of the world—violence, poverty, injustice—we are not speaking conceptually; we are talking about things that happen to bodies. When we say millions around the world are impacted by the global epidemic of famine, what we are saying is that millions of humans are experiencing the physical deterioration of muscle and other tissue due to lack of nutrients in their bodies. *Injustice* is an opaque word until we are willing to discuss its material reality as, for example, the three years sixteen-year-old Kalief Browder spent beaten and locked in solitary confinement in Riker's Island prison without ever being charged with a single crime. His suicide and his mother's heart attack two years later are not abstractions; they are the outcomes injustice enacted on two bodies.[4] Racism, sexism, ableism, homo- and transphobia, ageism, fatphobia are algorithms created by humans' struggle to make peace with the body. A radical self-love world is a world free from the systems of oppression that make it difficult and sometimes deadly to live in our bodies.

A radical self-love world is a world that works for every body. Creating such a world is an inside-out job. How we value and honor our own bodies impacts how we value and honor the bodies of others. Our own radical self-love reconnection is the blueprint for what author Charles Eisenstein calls *The More Beautiful World Our Hearts Know Is Possible.*[5] It is through our own transformed relationship with our bodies that we become champions for other bodies on our planet. As we awaken to our indoctrinated body shame, we feel inspired to awaken others and to interrupt the systems that perpetuate body shame and oppression against all bodies. There is a whisper we keep hearing; it is saying we must build in us what we want to see built in the world. When we act from this truth on a global scale, using the lens of the body, we usher in the transformative opportunity of radical self-love, which is the opportunity for a more just, equitable, and compassionate world for us all.

Moving from body shame to radical self-love is a road of inquiry and insight. We will need to ask ourselves tough questions from a place of grace and grounding. Together we will examine what we have come to believe about ourselves, our bodies, and the world we live in. At times, the road may appear dark and ominous, but fret not, my friend! I have provided some lampposts along the way. They come in the form of Unapologetic Inquiries, questions you will ask yourself as you endeavor to explore the mechanisms of your body shame and dismantle its parts. Radical Reflections will highlight central themes and concepts you will want to remember as we take this journey together. This is not a math test and you cannot fail. Be patient with yourself, take your time. As my best friend Maureen Benson says, "You are not late."[6]

Why Must It Be Radical?

"Okay, Sonya. I get it. Loving ourselves is important. But why do we have to be all radical about it?" To answer this question is to further distinguish radical self-love from its fickle cousins, self-confidence and self-esteem, or its scrappy kid sister, self-acceptance. It requires that we explore the definition of the word *radical*. Language is fluid and evolutionary, regularly leaving dictionary definitions feeling dated and sorely lacking in nuance. How we construct language is an enormous part of how we understand and judge bodies. The definition of *radical* is a powerful one as we explore its relationship to self-love. Dictionary.com defines *radical* as:

1. of or going to the root or origin; fundamental: a radical difference.
2. thoroughgoing or extreme, especially as regards change from accepted or traditional forms: a radical change in the policy of a company.
3. favoring drastic political, economic, or social reforms: radical ideas; radical and anarchistic ideologues.
4. forming a basis or foundation.
5. existing inherently in a thing or person: radical defects of character.[7]

Radical self-love is deeper, wider, and more expansive than anything we would call self-confidence or self-esteem. It is juicier than self-acceptance. Including the word *radical* offers us a self-love that is the root or origin of our relationship to ourselves. We did not start life in a negative partnership with our bodies. I have never seen a toddler lament the size of their thighs, the squishiness of their belly. Children do not arrive here ashamed of their race, gender, age, or differing abilities. Babies love their bodies! Each discovery they encounter is freaking awesome. Have you ever seen an infant realize they have feet? Talk about wonder! That is what an unobstructed relationship with our bodies looks like. You were an infant once, which means there was a time when you thought your body was freaking awesome too. Connecting to that memory may feel as distant as the farthest star. It may not be a memory you can access at all, but just knowing that there was a point in your history when you once loved your body can be a reminder that body shame is a fantastically crappy inheritance. We didn't give it to ourselves, and we are not obligated to keep it. We arrived on this planet as LOVE.

We need not do anything other than turn on a television for evidence affirming how desperately our society, our world, needs an extreme form of self-love to counter the constant barrage of shame, discrimination, and body-based oppression enacted against us daily. Television shows like *The Biggest Loser* encourage dangerous and unsustainable exercise and food restriction from their contestants while using their bodies as fodder for our entertainment and reinforcing the notion that the most undesirable body one can have is a fat body. Researchers have shown that American news outlets regularly exaggerate crime rates, including a tendency to inflate the rates of Black offenses while depicting Black suspects in a less favorable light than their White counterparts.[8] People with disabilities are virtually nonexistent on television unless they are being trotted out as "inspiration porn." Their stories are often told in ways that exploit their disabilities for the emotional edification of able-bodied people, presenting them as superhuman for doing unspectacular things like reading or going to the store or, worse yet, for overcoming obstacles placed on them by the very society that fails to acknowledge or appropriately accommodate their bodies.[9] *Of course* we need something radical to challenge these messages.

Using the term *radical* elevates the reality that our society requires a drastic political, economic, and social reformation in the ways in which we deal with bodies and body difference. The U.S. Constitution was written to sanction governmental body oppression. When the Bill of Rights was signed, relatively few Americans had voting rights.[10] Among those excluded from suffrage were African Americans, Native Americans, women, White men with disabilities, and White males who did not own land. Voting rights for women . . . nope. Blacks . . . nope; they were only counted as three-fifths of a full person. Using a wheelchair? No voting for you, dear. Race, gender, and disability prejudice were written into the governing documents of the United States.[11] Consider that the right to marry the person you love regardless of your gender was only legally sanctioned in the United States in 2015.[12] Out of 195 countries in the world, same-sex marriage is legal in only 30 of them.[13] Marriage equality for same-sex couples is in its historical infancy in the United States and nonexistent for most of the world. Transgender people are currently fighting across the United States to retain the legal right to use the bathroom that matches their gender identity.[14] People with disabilities have higher rates of unemployment regardless of educational attainment.[15]

These political, economic, and social issues are about our bodies. They intersect with our race, age, gender, ability, sexual orientation, and a multitude of other ways our bodies exist. In 1989, Columbia law professor and scholar Kimberlé Crenshaw gave a name to this long-understood dynamic. She called it *intersectionality* and defined it as:

> the study of overlapping or intersecting social identities and related systems of oppression, domination, or discrimination. The theory suggests that—and seeks to examine how—various biological, social, and cultural categories such as gender, race, class, ability, sexual orientation, religion, caste, age, and other axes of identity interact on multiple and often simultaneous levels. The theory proposes that we should think of each element or trait of a person as inextricably linked with all of the other elements in order to fully understand one's identity.[16]

Intersectionality has become a term often revered or repudiated depending on the source. Put plainly, none of us is mono-dimensional. We are not only men, fathers, people living with lupus, Asian, or seniors. Some of us are aging Asian fathers who are living with lupus. Those varying identities impact each other in ways that are significantly different than if we were navigating them one at a time. Radical self-love demands that we see ourselves and others in the fullness of our complexities and intersections and that we work to create space for those intersections. As has been true throughout history, changing the systemic and structural oppressions that regard us in perfunctory and myopic ways requires sweeping changes in our laws, policies, and social norms. Creating a world of justice for all bodies demands that we be radical and intersectional.

Unapologetic Inquiry #1

We all live at multiple intersections of identity. What are your intersections? How do your multiple identities affect each other?

Radical self-love is interdependent. The radical self-love es-
poused in this book lives beyond the flimsy ethos of individualism
and operates at both the individual and systemic levels. Radical self-
love is about the self because the self is part of the whole. And therefore, radical self-love is the foundation of radical human love. Our
relationships with our own bodies inform our relationships with
others. Consider all the times you have assessed your value or lack
thereof by comparing yourself to someone else. When we are saddled with body shame, we see other bodies as things to covet or
judge. Body shame makes us view bodies in narrow terms like
"good" or "bad," or "better" or "worse" than our own. Radical self-
love invites us to love our bodies in a way that transforms how we
understand and accept the bodies of others. This is not to say that
we magically like everyone. It simply means we have debates and
disagreements about ideas and character, not about bodies. When
we can see the obvious truth inherent in artist and activist Glen Mar-
la's quote, "There is no wrong way to have a body," we learn to love
bodies even when we don't like the humans inhabiting them.[17]

Our personal radical self-love transformation alters the workings
of the world. Model Cacsmy Brutus exemplified this principle in life.
Mama Cax, as she was known, was a Haitian-born Black woman di-
agnosed with osteosarcoma and lung cancer when she was fourteen
years old. A failed hip replacement after her cancer treatment forced
her to have her leg amputated, and for years after her amputation,
she tried to hide her prosthetic leg, her body shame spiraling into
years-long depression. On March 14, 2013, she posted a simple
photo on Instagram standing in a short yellow dress with her prosthetic leg unapologetically visible. The caption stated, "I read some-
where that freedom lies in being yourself. I hope you guys are free."
Cacsmy feared the world would meet the sight of her prosthetic leg
with pity, but instead her community heralded her as a "badass."
That small radical step illuminated a path toward her purpose that

would have remained obscured, camouflaged behind years of shame, if not for a series of small but life-altering acts. I came to know of Mama Cax in 2017 after she began her professional modeling career. She went from working in the New York mayor's office to being represented by a major New York modeling agency and walking in runway shows for Chromat and Rihanna's Fenty lingerie. She was bald and dark just like me, disabled and unapologetically so. She was a necessary brick in building a monument of radical self-love for the planet, and her choice to embrace her body, disabilities, and difference brought her out of the shadows and in front of hundreds of thousands of people who needed to know a Mama Cax was possible in the world. She not only transformed her life, she also contributed to a transformation in the visibility and accessibility of disabled bodies, Black bodies, immigrant bodies in careers previously blocked from them. Mama Cax in her radical majestic body played a key part in the diversity we currently see in the beauty and fashion industry. Be clear: these industries are nowhere near equitable and still primarily uphold impossible standards of beauty, but narratives about which bodies deserve to be seen and celebrated have begun shifting. We can feel the ground shaking beneath those impossible standards and in no small part because of what Mama Cax did to advance a new vision of beauty and power. Mama Cax died on December 16, 2019. She was just thirty years old. Her brief but mighty life is a reminder that our personal radical self-love journey is a stream inseparable from the ocean of change radical self-love makes possible.[18]

Unapologetic Inquiry #2

Can you recall an occasion when you compared yourself to someone? How did the comparison impact your self-esteem and self-confidence? How did it impact your ideas about the other person?

Radical self-love is indeed our inherent natural state, but social, political, and economic systems of oppression have distanced us from that knowing. Remember that toddler I mentioned a few paragraphs ago who delighted in their wondrous body—a.k.a. you as a kid? I know radical self-love can seem like a planet outside any galaxy you've heard of. I want to assure you: radical self-love is not light years away. It is not away at all. It lives in you. It is your very essence. You do not have to become radical self-love. You don't have to try to travel to it as though it were some far-off destination. Think of body shame like the layers of an onion. For decades in our own lives and for centuries in civilization, we have been taught to judge and shame our bodies and to consequently judge and shame others. Getting to our inherent state of radical self-love means peeling away those ancient, toxic messages about bodies. It is like returning the world's ugliest shame sweater back to the store where it was purchased and coming out wearing nothing but a birthday suit of radical self-love. By refusing to accept body shame as some natural consequence of being in a body, we can stop apologizing for our bodies and erase the distance between ourselves and radical self-love. When we do that, we are instantly returned to the radically self-loving stars we always were. Talk about a transformative power!

What Have We Been Apologizing For? What If We Stopped?

As a nine-year-old, I was sorry for everything. "Sonie, you left the refrigerator open!" "Sorry." "Sonya, why is your coat on the couch?" "Sorry." "Sonya, did you get grape jelly on that white pantsuit I paid good money for?" "Sorry, sorry, sorry . . ." A litany of apologies for my ever clumsy, messy, forgetful self, who spilled evidence of such all over the house. "Sorry" was my way of gathering up the spill. After all, I was a new generation of "raising kids" my grandmother was enlisted to do after having already raised three children on her own. I knew that my grandmother loved me, but even at nine years old I also knew she had to be exhausted. Grandma eventually started scolding me for saying *sorry* all the time. "Hush all that *sorry*. You ain't sorry. If you were sorry you would stop doing it!" I wondered if there was any truth to my grandmother's admonishment. If I were sorry, truly sorry, would I stop doing whatever *it* was? Could I?

Living in a female body, a Black body, an aging body, a fat body, a body with mental illness is to awaken daily to a planet that expects a certain set of apologies to already live on our tongues. There is a level of "not enough" or "too much" sewn into these strands of difference. Recent discoveries in the field of epigenetics have established how the traumas and resiliency of our ancestors are passed on to us molecularly.[19] Being sorry is literally a lesson in our DNA. In the Jim Crow South, an apology could at times be exacted by death sentence. Emmett Till's family came to know this brutal fact in the summer of 1955, when the fifteen-year-old's obligatory apology for whistling at a White woman would come in the form of a fatal gunshot after which his lifeless body was affixed to a tire and dumped in the Tallahatchie River.[20] For far too many women, the expectation of apology began after the sexual-assault report ended in an interrogation about the length of the skirt she was wearing or how many drinks she had at the party. There are minuscule daily ways each of us will be asked to apologize for our bodies, no matter how "normal" they appear. The conservative haircut needed to placate the new supervisor, the tattoo you cover when you step into an office building to increase your chances of being treated "professionally" are examples of tiny apologies society will ask you to render for being in your body as you see fit. For so many of us, *sorry* has become how we translate the word *body*.

Unapologetic Inquiry #3

In what ways have you been asked to apologize for your body?

For decades, I spread out before the world a buffet of apologies. I apologized for laughing too loudly, being too big, too dark, flamboyant, outspoken, analytical. I watched countless others roll out similar scrolls of contrition. We made these apologies because our bodies had disabilities and needed access. We made them because our bodies were aging and slower, because our gender identity was different than the sex we were assigned at birth and it confused strangers. We apologized for our weight, race, sexual orientation. We were told there is a right way to have a body, and our apologies reflected our indoctrination into that belief. We believed there was indeed a way in which our bodies were wrong. Not only have we been trying to change our "wrong bodies," but we have also continued to apologize for the presumed discomfort our bodies rouse in others. Whether we perceived ourselves as making the passenger beside us uncomfortable by taking up "too much" space in our airplane seat or we believed that our brown skin frightened the White woman who clutched her purse and crossed the street when she saw us approaching, either way it was in these moments that we found our heads bowed in shame, certain that our too fat, too dark, too muchness was the offense. It is never the failure of the seat or of its makers, who opted not to design it for myriad bodies. Of course, it is not our media companies' exaggeration of crime in communities of color that is culpable for planting the seeds of prejudice in so many citizens. We, at every turn, have decided that we are the culprits of our own victimization. However, not only are we constantly atoning; we have demanded our fair share of apologies from others as well. We, too, have snickered at the fat body at the beach, shamed the transgender body at the grocery store, pitied the disabled body while clothes shopping, maligned the aging body. We have demanded the apology from other bodies. We have ranked our bodies against the bodies of others, deciding they are greater or lesser than our own based on the prejudices and biases we inherited.

Dismantling the culture of apology requires an investigation into the anatomy of an apology. Generally, people committed to their righteousness rarely feel the need to apologize. About five years ago I shared with an ex how something he'd said had hurt my feelings. After twenty minutes of his dancing around any admission of offense, it became clear this guy was not planning to issue any apologies. According to his logic, he did not intend to hurt my feelings and therefore did not owe me an apology. Like many people, he felt that his intention should have absolved him from his impact. I countered his reasoning by asking, "If you accidently stepped on someone's foot, would you say *sorry?*" "No, not if their foot was the only place to stand," he replied matter-of-factly. (Why had I dated this guy?) Clearly, I do not propose that we, as a species, adopt this sort of thoughtless, self-centered ideology, but sometimes even jerks can lead us to epiphanies. There was something about his refusal to apologize for what he saw as taking up the space he needed that, if wielded authentically, might change how we move through the world.

In a conversation on a podcast called *Myelin and Melanin*, which highlights the unique challenges of being Black and living with multiple sclerosis, the host shared how for years she avoided using mobility aids such as canes or a wheelchair. She felt uncomfortable not only with the visibility of her disability but how such aids took up what she called "too much space." Take a moment to consider that space is actually infinite, right? The notion of "taking too much space" is born out of a framework of scarcity upon which we have built a world where some people are allowed to build skyscrapers and stadiums or run countries and make laws for the masses, while others are told to stay small, go unnoticed, don't take up too much room on the sidewalk. But only some of us receive that message. We have yet to collectively tell Amazon gazillionaire Jeff Bezos or Facebook founder Mark Zuckerberg, "Hey, buddy, you're just taking up too much space!"

Space is infinite and yet it is possible to be out of balance. With canyon-sized wealth gaps feeding global poverty but not bellies, billionaires are out of balance. Those of us who believe we do not have the "right body" spend decades of our life and dollars trying to shrink, tuck, and tame ourselves into the right body all the while forfeiting precious space on the planet because we don't feel entitled to it. We, too, are out of balance. Some of us have no problems taking up space (google *manspreading*), while others move closer to invisibility daily. I long for a mutiny of space. May there be ten million wheelchairs, canes, service dogs, and mobility aids on every street in every country. Let there be double seats for every fat body, and may every boardroom and decision-making entity be brimming with young and old, Black, Brown, and transgender bodies. Taking up space we have previously been denied is a step toward bringing a just balance of power and resources (i.e., space) in the world. It is an act of radical love.

Why are we constantly apologizing for the space we inhabit? What if we all understood the inherent vastness of our humanity and therefore occupied the world without apology? What if we all became committed to the idea that no one should have to apologize for being a human in a body? What if we made room for every body so that no one ever had to stand on someone else's foot? How might we change our lives? How might we change the world?

> **Radical Reflection**
> *Our freedom from body shame demands that we look at how we have perpetuated shame in others. We will need to be radically honest on this journey.*

Being a human can feel like a daunting task. It is easy to feel at the whim of the universe. We have been convinced we are ineffectual at exacting any real change against our social systems and structures, so instead we land the guilt and blame squarely on the shoulders of the most accessible party: ourselves. This burden has kept us immobile in our own lives and oblivious to our impact in the world. The weight of the shame has kept us small and trapped in the belief that our bodies and our lives are mistakes. What an exhausting and disheartening way to live. It was this sense of epic discouragement that fueled my inquiry into the nature of apology and led me to explore how our lives might look different if we began living unapologetically. What would the world look like if each of us navigated our lives with the total awareness that we owed no one an apology for our bodies? That exploration into unapologetic living led me to a two-tiered hypothesis. My hunch was, the more unapologetically I showed up in my body, in my community, my job, family, and world, one of two things would happen: either I would pass on to others the power and permission to be their unapologetic selves, or others would feel indicted and intimidated by my unapologetic being and would attempt to contain or shrink me. As the universe often does, it gave me the opportunity to test my hypothesis, in this case on the evening of February 9, 2011.

Six months prior, I had taken a camera-phone picture of myself in a black, strapless corset while getting dressed for an event. I was being saucy, sexy, and silly, and I absolutely did not think a single soul besides myself would ever lay eyes on that photo. For months, I'd catch myself skimming through images of old meals, museum visits, cute shoe fantasy purchases, and then I would happen upon the photo of my dark, wide body in the black corset. Damn, I was hot! And yet, despite feeling vibrant and bold, I was terrified to share the photo with anyone. The voices of apology immediately began a chorus of questions: Would people think I was vain? Would they fail to see the beautiful woman I saw in the image and instead simply remind me that I was too fat, too Black, too queer, too woman, and no one was ever going to think that was beautiful? Unable to answer my litany of shame-based interrogations, the photo remained secreted away in my cell phone, only spied when I needed an esteem boost (see how my self-esteem was floating at sea, buoyed only by a selfie).

A war I could not yet name was raging inside me. It was the war between radical self-love and body shame. On February 9, 2011, a friend posted a picture of plus-size model Tara Lynn on my Facebook wall. Immediately I was taken aback by her gorgeousness and more than a little enamored (read: total crush). Searching her name on Google (a.k.a. Internet scrolling through her pics for hours) returned photo after photo of this stunning woman posing casually in jeans and a crisp white shirt for a trendy department store or wearing nothing but a string of pearls while splayed across a fur rug. But the final photo would be the one to prove at least a portion of my hypothesis. I ran the mouse across the hyperlink, and there was Tara Lynn standing resplendent in a black corset, the cover girl for a new lingerie campaign.[21] Her empowered being instantly empowered my being. In one click of a digital image, Tara Lynn gave me permission to be fully seen in my body, opinions be damned! I did in that moment what I had felt completely incapable of doing for months: I immediately posted the picture of me in my black corset to Facebook. Alongside the image I wrote the following caption: "In this picture, I am 230 lbs. In this picture, I have stretch marks and an unfortunate decision in the shape of

> **Radical Reflection**
>
> *The voice of doubt, shame, and guilt blaring in our heads is not our voice. It is a voice we have been given by a society steeped in shame. It is the "outside voice." Our authentic voice, our "inside voice," is the voice of radical self-love!*

a melting Hershey's Kiss on my left thigh. I am smiling, like a woman who knows you're watching and likes it. For this one camera flash, I am unashamed, unapologetic."[22]

Just as Tara Lynn's unapologetic power permissioned my own, I did the same for others, asking my friends to share photos in which they felt unashamed and unapologetic in their bodies. The next morning I opened my Facebook page only to discover I had been tagged in over thirty photos of people of varying ages, races, sizes, abilities, genders, sexual orientations, and more who had chosen, even if just for that brief minute, to stop hiding and apologizing and instead simply be their unabashed selves. I was consumed. I needed to know the bounds of this unmapped universe where all of us could live in our bodies like we knew we were already okay. Aware that I would need other unapologetic people willing to explore this budding notion with me, I did what any Gen Xer on the cusp of millennial status would do: I started a Facebook group and used it to house these newly sourced unapologetic photos from my friends around the country. The group operated as a geographically unconstrained space where we could practice loving ourselves, our bodies, and other people's bodies unapologetically. I named the page after a poem I had written right around the time I took that fateful saucy selfie: "The Body Is Not an Apology." Quickly it became clear that our brief moments of unapologetic living were highly contagious acts—like the flu but much happier!

Being unapologetic created an opening for radical self-love. Each time we chose to embrace the fullness of ourselves, some layer of the body-shame onion got peeled away, evidencing the power of every small unapologetic act. I have been watching this radical disrobing of shame change the world, one unapologetic human at a time. And each moment that I practice living unapologetically I realize my grandma was right: I wasn't ever actually sorry. When we genuinely love ourselves, there is no need to be.

Unapologetic Inquiry #4

What are you ready to stop apologizing for?

The Three Peaces

From the moment the phrase "The body is not an apology" and the idea of radical self-love fell from my lips, they have echoed as a resounding "Yes!" to those who have heard them. That YES feeling is likely the reason you are reading this book right now. On some cellular level, we know our bodies are not something we should apologize for. After all, they are the only way we get to experience this ridiculous and radiant life. A part of us is a bit repelled by the overt espousal of body shame. It is the reason we whisper and rumor about other folks' bodies behind their backs. We know our snickers and taunts are wrong. When we are honest with ourselves, we feel gross about the way we vulture other humans, picking apart their bodies, consuming them for the sake of our own fragile sense of self. We feel gross when we think about all the vicious, cruel comments we've heard leveled against people's bodies; comments spoken around us without a single protest from us.

Our best selves find the evisceration of other humans repugnant. We feel shame when we are shamed. And when we allow ourselves, we feel shame for having shamed others. Feelings of shame suck! So, what do we do? Stop shaming people? No. We distance ourselves from the guilt by couching our body judgment in the convenient container of choice. We say things like, "Hey, it's okay to judge them; they chose to be gay." "You know you could lose weight if you wanted to!" "It's not my fault you are a guy dressing like a girl!"

The argument that people "chose" to be this way or the other is at its core an argument about difference and our inability to understand and make peace with difference. The notion of choice is a convenient scapegoat for our bias and bigotries. Logic says, "If people are choosing to be different, they can just as simply choose to be the way I believe they should be." What we must ask ourselves instead is, "Why do I need people to be the way I believe they should be?" The argument about choice is a projection. There are endless things in the world we do not understand, and yet we live in a culture where we are expected to know and understand everything! Humans are rarely given permission to not understand without someone calling us failures or stupid. No one wants to feel like a stupid failure, and our brains have all sorts of savvy tricks to avoid those feelings.

A particularly strategic maneuver is to decide that if we don't understand something it must be wrong. After all, wrong is simpler than not knowing. Wrong means I am not stupid or failing. See all that sneaky, slimy projection happening there? Projection shields us from personal responsibility. It obscures our shame and confusion and places the onus for reconciling it on the body of someone else. We don't have to work to understand something when it is someone else's fault. We don't have to undo the shame-based beliefs we were brought up with. We don't have to question our parents, friends, churches, synagogues, mosques, government, media. We don't have to challenge or be challenged. When we decide that people's bodies are wrong because we don't understand them, we are trying to avoid the discomfort of divesting from an entire body-shame system.

How do we fight the impetus to make the bodies we do not understand wrong? There are three key tenets that will help pry us out of the mire of body judgment and shame. I call them the Three Peaces. They are:

1. Make peace with not understanding.
2. Make peace with difference.
3. Make peace with *your* body.

Peace with Not Understanding

We must make peace with not understanding. Understanding is not a prerequisite for honor, love, or respect. I know extraordinarily little about the stars, but I honor their beauty. I know virtually nothing about black holes, but I respect their incomprehensible power. I do not understand the shelf life of Twinkies, but I love them and pray there be an endless supply in the event of an apocalypse! When we liberate ourselves from the expectation that we must have all things figured out, we enter a sanctuary of empathy. Being uncertain, lacking information, or simply not knowing something ought not be an indictment against our intelligence or value. Lots of exceptionally smart people can't work a copy machine. This is not about smarts. Nor am I proposing we eschew information. Quite to the contrary, this is an invitation to curiosity. Not knowing is an opportunity for exploration without judgment and demands. It leaves room for the possibility that we might conduct all manner of investigation, and after said research is completed we may still not "get it." Whatever "it" may be. Understanding is ideal, but it is not an essential ingredient for making peace. Buddhist teachings tell us that the alleviation of suffering is achieved through the act of acceptance.[23] Here is a place where acceptance becomes a tool of expansion. Genuine acceptance invites reality without resistance. Wrong and right are statements of resistance and are useless when directed at people's bodies. "Her thin body is just wrong" sounds nonsensical because beneath our many layers of body shame, we know that bodies are neither wrong nor right. They just are.

Acceptance should not be confused with compliance or the proposal that we must be resigned to the ills and violence of the world. We should not. But we must be clear that people's bodies are not the cause of our social maladies. Napoleon was not a tyrant because he was short. Osama bin Laden was not a terrorist because Muslims are predisposed to violence. Our disconnection, trauma, lack of resources, lack of compassion, fear, greed, and ego are the sources of our contributions to human suffering, not our bodies. We can accept humans and their bodies without understanding why they love, think, move, or look the way they do. Contrary to common opinion, freeing ourselves from the need to understand everything can bring about a tremendous amount of peace.

Unapologetic Inquiry #5

What are you willing to stop struggling to understand for the sake of peace?

Peace with Difference

We must make peace with difference. This is a simple perspective when applied to nature, but oh, how we struggle when transferring the concept onto human forms. The late poet and activist Audre Lorde said, "It is not our differences that divide us. It is our inability to recognize, accept, and celebrate those differences."[24] Think of all the times we have heard some well-meaning person attempting to usher in social harmony by declaring, "But aren't we all the same?" Here's the short answer to that: No. We are not all the same, no more than every tree is the same or every houseplant or dog. Humans are a complicated and varied bunch, and those variations impact our lived experiences. The idea that we are all the same is often a mask. It is what we tell ourselves when we haven't mastered the first Peace. Rather than owning that we don't understand someone's experience, we shrink it or stuff it into our tiny capsules of knowledge. We homogenize it by proclaiming we are all the same.

Dr. Deb Burgard, a renowned eating disorders therapist and pioneer in the Health at Every Size (HAES)[25] movement, cocreated a brilliant animated video called "The Danger of Poodle Science" to explain body diversity and the perils of assessing health and wellness based on assumptions about size.[26] In it, Dr. Burgard details how absurd it would be if we assessed the health of all dogs by comparing them to the size and health of poodles. Better yet, what if the poodles decided that all other dogs should look, eat, and be the same size as poodles? The video pokes fun at our medical industry and its one-size-fits-all orientation toward bodies. Rather than acknowledging and basing research on the premise that diversity in weight and size are natural occurrences in humans, we treat larger bodies with poodle science and then pathologize those bodies by using the rhetoric of health. "I just want this complete stranger, whose life I know nothing about and whom I have made no effort to get to know beyond this Twitter thread, to be healthy." This is called health trolling or concern trolling, and it is just another sinister body shame tactic. Given that we can make no accurate assessment of any individual's health based simply on their weight (or photo on social media), it is evident that such behavior is not really about the person's health but more likely about the ways in which we expect other bodies to conform to our standards and beliefs about what a body should or should not look like. Equally damaging is our insistence that all bodies should be healthy. Health is not a state we owe the world. We are not less valuable, worthy, or lovable because we are not healthy. Lastly, there is no standard of health that is achievable for all bodies. Our belief that there should be anchors the systemic oppression of ableism and reinforces the notion that people with illnesses and disabilities have defective bodies rather than different bodies. Each of us will have varying degrees of health and wellness throughout our lives, and our arbitrary demands and expectations as they relate to the health and size of people's bodies fuel inequality and injustice.

Not only do such demands perpetuate injustice, much of the "science" put forth regarding weight and health was born out of systems of inequity. In Sabrina Strings's 2018 release *Fearing the Black Body:*

The Racial Origins of Fat Phobia she traces the beginnings of our fear of fat bodies back to the proliferation of Protestant religious dogma in North America and African chattel slave trade, offering that not until theology converged with an influx of African bodies in America did fatness become part of a medicalized public health ideology. She states, "The phobia about fatness and the preference for thinness have not, principally or historically, been about health. Instead, they have been one way the body has been used to craft and legitimate race, sex, and class hierarchies."[27] Start by remembering everyone is not a poodle, and that is okay. Boy, would the world be a boring, yappy place if we all were.

Bodies are diverse not only in size but in race and ethnicity, sexual orientation, gender, physical ability, and mental health. The example of poodle science speaks to a larger issue, one in which our societies have defined what is considered a normal body and have assigned greater value, resources, and opportunities to the bodies most closely aligned with those ideas of normal. When we propose that all bodies are the same, we also propose that there is a standard to measure sameness against. I call this standard the "default body." Aspects of the default body change across culture and geography, but it shapes our ideas of normalcy and impacts our social values.

Our assumptions about the default identities of race, age, ability, sexual orientation, gender, size, and so on become the bedrock upon which societies build body-based oppression. We will explore later how our notions of default bodies developed over time, but for now just know that our propensity to shrink human diversity into sameness creates barriers for

> **Radical Reflection**
> *"Celebrating difference" is nice but not transformative. It is constrained by the boundaries of our imaginations. We must strive to create a difference-celebrating culture where we see diversity as an intrinsic part of our everyday lives.*

the bodies that do not fit our default models. We must move from occasionally celebrating difference (as long as it doesn't fall too far outside the boundaries of our ideas of "normal") to developing a difference-celebrating culture. Inequality and injustice rest firmly on our unwillingness to exalt the vast magnificence of the human body.

Unapologetic Inquiry #6

In what ways have you tried to make other people "the same" as you? What parts of their identity did you erase by doing this?

Peace with Your Body

Lastly, you must make peace with *your* body. I have been talking all kumbaya and collective in the first two Peaces, but this one is all on you, love. Your body is the body it is. Your belief that your body should be some other body other than the body it is is likely a reflection of your struggles with the first two Peaces. As I said at the beginning of the book, you did not come to the planet hating your body. What if you accepted the fact that much of how you view your body and your judgments of it are learned things, messages you have deeply internalized that have created an adversarial relationship? Hating your body is like finding a person you despise and then choosing to spend the rest of your life with them while loathing every moment of the partnership. I know that lots of humans stay in loveless commitments. Not only am I proposing that you should not stay in a loveless partnership; I am also proposing that your partner has been set up. If your body were an episode of *Law and Order: Special Victims Unit*, it would be getting framed for crimes it did not commit. Get out of that damn television show and into living in peace and harmony with the body you have today. Your body need not be a prison sentence. And if you are living in it as such, I am glad you picked up this book. As they say in the tradition of twelve-step programs, "You are in the right place."[28]

I am not simply proposing that you make peace with your body because your body shame is making you miserable. I am proposing you do it because it's making us miserable too. Your children are sad that they have no photos with you. Your teenager is wondering if they, too, will be obligated to hate their body because they see you hating yours. The bodies you share space with are afraid you are judging them with the same venom they have watched you use to judge yourself. Remember that body shame is as contagious as radical self-love. Making peace with your body is your mighty act of revolution. It is your contribution to a changed planet where we might all live unapologetically in the bodies we have.

Unapologetic Inquiry #7

Who in your life is most affected by your body shame? How is it impacting them?

I know you may be saying, "But I don't know how to make peace with my body!" On these pages, together, we are going to help you master the third Peace. The key to getting out of a maze is remembering the way you got in. It's not an easy task, but this book is an attempt to start at the beginning and show you how you got to the center of body shame. Together we are going to walk back to the beginning and out of the maze. Radical self-love is both the light that will guide us and the gift on the other side.

Radical Reflection

Spend some time reflecting on Chapter 1. Notice what fears or concerns it triggers in you. Notice where there is excitement or joy. Share both with a friend.

2

Shame, Guilt, and Apology— Then and Now

When Did We Learn to Hate Them?

"Keisha Bald Spots!" was the consistent choral offering on Keisha's brief bus ride to Woolslair Elementary School. The teasing was brutal and regular, but in some ways the daily routine made it easier to adapt to. Keisha's mama had a penchant for gorgeous, labyrinthine braided hairstyles. Her mother also had the grip of an X-Men character, and by the time Keisha was in third grade the tight braids had ripped her hair right out of her nine-year-old scalp, causing permanent bald spots on both sides of her head, a condition known as traction alopecia. Being different is difficult in a world that tells us there is a normal. Many of us have oriented our entire lives around an effort to be normal, never realizing that normal is not a stationary goal. It keeps moving while we dance a perpetual foxtrot, jitterbug, and paso doble around it, trying to catch up and confused when we finish each day exhausted and uninspired by this party called life.

It is considered normal for women and girls in the United States to have hair, a reality shaped to varying degrees by the default of westernized beauty standards. In Western societies, hair is often tied to notions of femininity, beauty, and gender. Having hair is what is expected of a "normal" woman or girl. Of course, there is an endless screed of rules governing our notions of normal hair. One cannot have too much hair or too little. Hair can only be in certain places on our bodies. Hair should have a certain texture, should be a certain color. For Americans, the rules for hair (like most of our body rules) come with a default aesthetic: long, straight, fine . . . and, if possible, blond.

Even before the children on the school bus began singing "Keisha! Keisha Bald Spots!" it is likely that Keisha already knew she did not fit the default of normal hair. Commercials would have told her, music would have said it, pictures in her schoolbooks would have made it clear that Keisha's hair was not the default. Her short, dark, kinky hair and soon-to-be partially bald head would never be the default and by extension never normal. Both subtly and overtly, Keisha experienced the body terrorism of White supremacy, and was learning to see her own Black features as abnormal and thereby ugly. In our society, normal is the pathway to worthy and beautiful.

Body-Shame Origin Stories

If I asked you to recall your first memory of body shame, it is likely that your story, like Keisha's, would have at least one of the following elements:

- Developed in your youth
- Was a response to rapid or unexpected body change
- Occurred when you became aware of difference
- Led you to assume there was some "should" about your body
- Was reflected or enforced by familial, social, cultural, and political messaging and systems of body-based oppression
- Was attached to a story or belief about your value and worth in the world

Having traveled the country and listened to thousands of body-shame stories, I observed patterns that elucidated how our indoctrination into body shame shares some key characteristics. For many of us, our first shame memories occur before we even enter our teenage years. It is unsurprising that early on we internalize these negative messages. Being young and particularly impressionable, we take cues from the external world about who we are and who we should be. In childhood, when we are highly impressionable and in the infancy of developing a sense of individuation and identity, it is no surprise that the earliest seeds of body shame might begin to take root. A Yahoo Health survey of 1,993 teen and adult respondents found that the average age of body-shame consciousness was between thirteen and fourteen. Additionally, it found that respondents were experiencing body shame at increasingly younger ages, some beginning at nine and ten.[1] In the workshops on radical self-love offered by The Body Is Not an Apology, participants are asked to share their earliest memories of body shame.[2] Here are some responses:

> *I was around seven years old and a little boy in school, named James, called me fat. I think that was when I started dieting.*
>
> -KATHLEEN

> *At about age seven, the older brother of a friend told me girls couldn't go topless because it was dirty.*
>
> -EMMA

> *I was four years old, my first day at daycare, and a little boy [told] me I looked like a bulldog.*
>
> -AMY

For Keisha, Kathleen, Emma, and Amy, those early messages stuck with them and shaped their sense of worth and value. The messages altered how they felt about their bodies. Girls are by no means the only ones receiving these detrimental messages. Boys, trans children, and gender-nonconforming children receive similar shaming messages in their early years.[3]

> *I was twelve years old when my basketball teammates and I were changing in the locker room. One of the kids called me chicken chest because I was so skinny. My team made clucking noises at me for the rest of the season.*
>
> -DAVID

> *From the age of six I knew I felt like a boy. I hated the dresses and dolls my mother forced on me. Whenever I complained, she'd tell me as long as she bought the clothes, I would wear what she told me to. I learned quickly that who I was was not okay.*
>
> -ALEX

Unapologetic Inquiry #8

What is your earliest memory of body shame? How is it similar to or different from the other stories shared here?

Our seminal experiences of body shame are often a result of some rapid or noticeable change in our physical selves. Nia was my childhood playmate and neighbor who lived in the same court of townhouses in East Liberty, a working-class neighborhood in my hometown of Pittsburgh, Pennsylvania. Nia was a few years older than the rest of the kids on my block and the first to be visited by the puberty fairy. On a sweaty July afternoon, while Nia, I, and several of the neighborhood kids beat the midday pavement in a rousing game of red light/green light, the adults were loudly scrutinizing our clumsy, gangly child bodies. Looking us over with equal parts marvel and pity, my two aunts and Nia's mother demanded, "Nia, come here. Are those bee stings, Nia?" My eldest aunt snickered. "Yup, looks like she's been stung," my younger aunt cackled. "Mmm-hmm, she been stung, and I just don't know what I am gonna do with her now!" chided her mother. My ten-year-old self was seriously confused. Why wasn't Nia crying after being stung by a bee? I always cried when that happened. Was it a special bee that didn't hurt? And even more confusing were the adults. Why were the grown folks laughing at her and being weird instead of helping her? Within moments it clicked. No one was discussing an insect-inflicted injury; they were poking fun at Nia's . . . gasp . . . boobies! Ten-year-old Sonya was mortified! Of course, if I could figure out this not-so-inside joke, certainly the eight other kids milling about would be in on the comedy soon enough. And my God, would this be what happened to me when I got the dreaded bee stings? In a mere five minutes, I had run through every embarrassing disaster scenario my puberty might elicit from the surrounding adults, all while poor Nia fled the scene, retreating to her home. I saw Nia just a few times the rest of the summer. I think she was hiding. From that moment forward, puberty became synonymous with public humiliation. I learned that

> ### Radical Reflection
> *Children's bodies are not public property. Teaching children bodily autonomy, privacy, and consent are the cornerstones of raising radical self-love humans.*

our bodies and their changes were areas of public domain—and things to broadcast, be teased about, be ashamed of.

Can you recall the messages you received about your own rapidly changing body during puberty? For all its everydayness, puberty is hard when you are a kid, even for those of us with experiences the world might call "normal." To understand the scope and range of body shame, we must consider what navigating the already treacherous terrain of rapid body change might be like for bodies that do not fit the definition of normal. What of the child whose gender identity does not match the changes their body is experiencing during puberty? What of the child navigating puberty in a fat body or a body with chronic illness? Our experiences of body shame are layered upon and impacted by the intersections of our identities. The less "normal" our identity, the more fraught the waters of body shame. Research shows that nearly 50 percent of transgender youth have seriously thought about suicide, and 25 percent report that they have made a suicide attempt.[4] How we are treated during puberty can be not only life-altering but life-threatening for some young people. As we consider our own body-shame origin story, we have potent access to a deeper empathy for all bodies.

Body shame is often a result of our burgeoning consciousness about our own difference. Whew, we sure do have a long-standing battle with our difference. Our first encounter with noticing our difference might have been when Billy in second grade pointed out that we had the biggest schnozzle . . . ahem . . . nose in the class. Maybe that consciousness came into focus with the awareness of our racial or sexual identities. Humans struggle with that second Peace. Part of our evolutionary success can be attributed to our skill at quickly assessing danger. "Nope, that is not a person; that is a boa constrictor!" See, quick! In an evolutionary sense, humans' ability to discern difference ensured that we stayed near the top of the food chain. Whereas noticing difference was historically necessary, modern humans have continued to use difference to sort ourselves, conflating difference with danger. Our rapid assessment of difference can be understood through a psychosocial dynamic called "in-group out-group bias." In 1982, researcher Henri Tajfel divided people into two random groups. He found that people began to favor their random group over people in the other random group (emphasis on *random*), at times even rationalizing reasons for the other group's immorality or poor character to justify disliking them.[5] Our ancient ancestors' battles for resources, food, even mates ensured that humans needed to find ways to identify who was part of their tribe and who was not. This in-group out-group distinction also meant that those outside our group were seen as a threat to our resources. The modern evolution of in-group out-group bias has been codified into our political, economic, and social systems. It has organized our world into a matrix of oppressive structures. But it doesn't have to stay that way. Ultimately we are wired to recognize difference and maybe even distrust it. However, we were also wired to eat bugs and to poop in a hole in the ground. The point being, we are capable of change. Seeing difference as synonymous with danger is an aspect of our social evolution that can and should be shifted. But we must grapple with difference. Our attempts to mute it reinforce the idea that difference is inherently bad.

Unapologetic Inquiry #9

When was the first time you noticed that you or someone else was different? What did you make the difference mean about you? What did you make it mean about them?

A year or so ago, a woman in one of my workshops shared that as a darker-skinned Black ballerina, she felt, from early in her training, as if something were holding her back. Eventually she concluded that it was the color of her skin. What might make this young woman feel as if her Blackness was a disadvantage in her pursuits as a classical dancer? Consider this hypothesis: when we don't see ourselves reflected in the world around us, we make judgments about that absence. Invisibility is a statement. It says something about the world and our place in it. A 2014 MTV study done in collaboration with David Binder Research found that among millennials, 73 percent of respondents believed that never considering race would improve society.[6] Unfortunately, despite our dreams of a utopic, color-blind planet, this thinking only functions to reinforce body shame. How many times have we heard or said, "I don't see color"? Although well-intentioned, not seeing color is ultimately a reflection of our personal challenges around navigating difference.

We may be trying to convey how we don't judge people based on racial identity, but "color blindness" is an act of erasure. Not only does it make invisible all the experiences a person has had that were shaped by their racial identity or color, it implies that to truly respect another human being we must obscure their areas of difference. Remember that we live in a world of default bodies, the bodies we imagine when we close our eyes. The default body becomes the template for the normal body. The only reason we would need to erase someone's difference is because we still equate difference with danger or undesirability. When we say we don't see color, what we are truly saying is, "I don't want to see the things about you that are different because society has told me they are dangerous or undesirable." Ignoring difference does not change society nor does it change the experiences non-normative bodies must navigate to survive. Rendering difference invisible validates the notion that there are parts of us that should be ignored, hidden, or minimized, leaving in place the unspoken idea that difference is the problem and not our approach to dealing with difference. Proposing that humans are all the same leaves the idea of the default body uninterrogated in our subconscious and firmly in place in our world, forcing all other bodies to conform or be rendered invisible.

Unapologetic Inquiry #10

Have you ever said any of the following? "I don't see color." "We are all the same." "I don't care if a person is white, black, purple, or whatever." "They are playing the 'race card.'" Considering this passage, what might you say next time?

Adults reinforce the message that different is bad by encouraging children to minimize difference or shaming them when they point it out. Diane, one of my workshop participants, recalled an incident in a grocery store when she went to pick up some vegetables for dinner. She encountered a woman and her four-year-old in the aisle directly in front of Diane's electric wheelchair. Diane was preparing to ask them to move over so that she could get to the eggplants when the woman's child began to point and squeal. Diane imagined that the child was responding not only to her apparent difference but also to her chair. The child's motioning and repetition of the phrase "Momma, it's an elecwic car!" suggested that Diane's chair perhaps looked like a toy car to the young child. All this deduction happened within a few seconds before the humiliated mother scolded the child for pointing and rushed off, never even acknowledging Diane's presence. Diane was disappointed. What could have been a powerful teaching opportunity turned into a mother reinforcing the notion that difference is not to be acknowledged. That child likely left the encounter feeling as if they had done something very wrong by openly noticing Diane. The child also left thinking that electric wheelchairs are toys. Inadvertently, the mother's actions conveyed the message that if bodies look different or move differently, we should not acknowledge that difference.

The most distressing message in Diane's encounter was the unintentional but deeply harmful one that disabled bodies should be ignored. When we fail to acknowledge Diane's difference, we also fail to account for or accommodate it. In this, we uphold the system of ableism, where able-bodied people are the default body and the world is constructed to best serve them at the expense of disabled people. Every message we receive as children tells us something not only about our own bodies but also about the bodies of others. How we treat difference and how we explain it to children can either reinforce the notions of body-based hierarchies or dismantle them. When we explore our assumptions about the bodies of others, we are better able to see where our defaults hinder the full range of human identity.

> ### Unapologetic Inquiry #11
>
> *Take a moment and think about the story of Diane and the mother and child at the grocery store. Consider what defaults you may have subconsciously assigned to the people in the story. Did you racialize them? If so, what races did you make them? Did you give the child a gender? Did you assume that the mother and child were able-bodied? Did they have large or small bodies?*

This exploration of how we assign default bodies is connected to our origins of body shame and the formation of the dreaded *should*. Our earliest memories of body shame left us with a sense that something was wrong with us, that our bodies should be different than they were (while consequently being the same as the other bodies around us). How we decided what our bodies should look like was formed in part by the messages we received. Those messages were transmitted and reinforced by culture, society, politics, and our families. Those messages stuck with us. "In a national survey of girls age 13 to 17 by the Girl Scouts Research Institute (2010), nearly half (48%) wished they were as skinny as the models they saw in fashion magazines and said fashion magazines gave them a body image to strive for (47%). Another survey by the Today Show and AOL.com (2014) found that 80% of teen girls compare themselves to images they see of celebrities, and, within that group, almost half say the images make them feel dissatisfied with the way they look."[7]

Confusing and stifling social messages about our bodies and identities transcend gender. Daemon, one of only a handful of male participants at my workshop, recalled his first memory of body shame at eight years old. He took a hard tumble off a merry-go-round at the local playground and scraped his knee badly. Bloodied and crying, he ran to his teenage and twenty-something cousins, who were supervising the smaller kids at the park. They immediately met his tears with laughter and taunting. The eldest cousin admonished, "Man up, dude! Only sissies cry." Daemon was clear that the brief but impactful moment changed him; he shared how he had not cried since he was eight years old. In those few brief moments, Daemon's cousins taught him that "man up" meant he must ignore both physical and emotional pain to be considered a man. His tears were bad and his pain inconsequential. Cultural and familial messages that reduce masculinity to a bland soup of physical strength and stoic emotional response limit the full range of human expression needed for boys to develop a healthy sense of radical self-love. We call these dangerous ideas "toxic masculinity."[8] Specifically, narratives that reinforce masculinity as synonymous with muscles can lead young men to "crash diets, over-exercising, smoking, increased drug and alcohol use or even taking dangerous supplements."[9] For Daemon, it led to years of ignoring his body, avoiding doctors, and masking pain with drugs and alcohol. Daemon said, "Having a stroke at thirty-seven was my wake-up call. If this was being a man, I was ready for a new definition." Cultural and social missives about who we are supposed to be and how our bodies are supposed to look are woven into the fabric of our daily lives, and whether we want to admit it or not, they impact our sense of self, often for decades to come. They become part of a larger story.

Let's return to Keisha for a moment. Can we see how the messages she received about her hair were cultural, social, and familial? Keisha recounted this story of shame in a workshop twenty-five years later, her voice still a cracked egg. I listened as she shared how she had felt unattractive and unlovable for nearly three decades, all because of her hair. It was clear that Keisha was moving through the world with her body-shame origin story still echoing against the walls of her life. She still lived in the shame of her story. The question is, in what ways are you?

One of the most impactful, difficult, and underexplored ways we form early messages about our bodies is a result of abuse and trauma. Not only have we grown up in societies that shame difference and judge by the metric of body-based oppression, but many of us grew up navigating personal physical and sexual harm. These memories can shape how we understand touch, pleasure, pain, and whether we experience our bodies as sites of safety or danger. When physical and sexual abuse happen in our childhoods, we are far more likely to personalize the harm, believing we must have done something to cause it. Survivors of abuse may often come to see their bodies as bad or wrong, blaming themselves and their physical form for the violations they endured. This internalization can set survivors on a lifetime path of body shame. In Black feminist scholar bell hooks's book *All about Love*, she notes, "Abused children have been taught that love can coexist with abuse. This shapes our adult perceptions of love. As we would cling to the notion that those who hurt us as children loved us, we rationalize being hurt by other adults by insisting that they love us."[10] These rationalizations do not only apply to the relationships we have with those who hurt us in the past and present. They can also characterize how we relate to and practice loving ourselves. We may justify our self-abuse and self-loathing by proclaiming it as "just the way it is," seeing abuse, neglect, and hurt as inevitable both externally and internally. Radical self-love returns accountability for the harm done to us back to the perpetrator and invites us to reclaim our victorious bodies. With radical self-love, we welcome what may feel like an entirely new possibility, one that author and pleasure activist adrienne maree brown encapsulates perfectly when she says, "I touch my own skin, and it tells me that before there was any harm, there was miracle."[11]

Unapologetic Inquiry #12

How are your early memories of body shame impacting your life today? What do you find yourself doing or not doing as a result of the shame?

Media Matters

At this point in our journey together you are likely to be experiencing one of two states. The first is a condition one of my workshop participants called "meta-shame." This is the state of feeling shame for feeling shame about our bodies. Doesn't it sound exhausting? It is!

In this blossoming age of "body positivity," it is trendy to profess our undying body love. We treat body positivity as though it is a trophy we can only receive when we reach some state of self-love enlightenment. Body shame is about as unfashionable as the rollers and bathrobe my mother would occasionally pick me up from school wearing, and yet for so many of us it is still our truth. It can be maddening when we see the ways in which we remain stuck on the carousel of our negative beliefs about default bodies and difference. We rage at ourselves about why we can't seem to crack the clay of body shame. Across the landscape of our existence we see its ravages everywhere and feel acutely conscious of all the glorious chances we have not taken because of it. We ache for all the opportunities we ignored. Splattered before us like bugs on the windshield of life are all the ways we have shrunk the full expression of ourselves because we have been convinced that our bodies and therefore our very beings are deficient. We can also see how our inability to get out of our shame story amplifies our feelings of inadequacy. Our presumed failure at attaining some body-love nirvana becomes just another source of shame.

The second state might involve an unexpected hankering to track down and curse Curtis from fifth grade who teased you to the point of tears. You are feeling certain he is the source of your body woes! Maybe you are blaming your mother who scolded you every time you reached for dessert after dinner. Yes! She is to blame! It is not surprising that these folks seem like malevolent perpetrators responsible for our years of body hatred and shame. But before you unleash the radical self-love army of vengeance upon their heads, you should know... there is no radical self-love army of vengeance.

> **Radical Reflection**
>
> *Avoid meta-shame, which is shame for having so much shame. Take a deep breath of kindness for yourself and your history of body shame/shaming. We can only do what we know. As famed poet Maya Angelou says, "When we know better, we do better." We can do better by giving ourselves more love.*

You should also know that although Curtis and your mother may indeed have helped you cultivate some awful beliefs about your body, they were not the authors of your body shame. Nor are you failing at body positivity. You, your mama, and Curtis have merely been pawns in a much longer and larger game of how we have all come to understand, judge, value, or devalue our bodies and the bodies of others.

Relationships with our bodies are social, political, and economic inheritances. The nature of these inheritances has changed over time, the default body morphing and transforming to suit the power structures of the day. We have not always seen fat bodies as less valuable. Throughout periods of human history, we have seen larger bodies not as markers of laziness or ill health but rather as representative of a life of wellness, wealth, and ease—something to aspire to. A larger body was representative of aristocracy and affluence. Fatness was all the rage for a while.[12] Gender and gender roles have also shifted over time, bending to fit the needs of the society. In 1479

B.C.E., Hatshepsut ascended to the throne of Egypt while donning male clothing and a beard to symbolize her intention to rule as a pharaoh.[13] Not all cultures have seen gender through rigid assignments of male or female. Indigenous cultures around the world have long accepted the concept of "two-spirit" people: those who embody both feminine and masculine identities or whose gender is more complicated than one of two options.[14] There were periods of time in history when the constructs of race looked considerably different. Irish folks were not enfolded into Whiteness when they arrived in America; neither were the Polish or Italians.[15] These elements of our identities are socially constructed and transmitted through a multitude of vehicles, including family, community, and culture. But no vehicle has been as potent in shaping our perceptions of bodies on a global scale as the vehicle of media.

Today we turn on the television or Netflix to watch our favorite series. Listen to satellite radio as we drive to work. Read the newspaper at lunch or scroll through the headlines populating our social media timelines. The many forms of media we interact with are ubiquitous entities informing nearly every aspect of our daily lives. Their pervasiveness and our rapid access

> **Radical Reflection**
> *All our body rules are made up!*

to them seem almost like science fiction (these days, something out of a dystopian novel), but forms of mass media have always existed, merely adapting and expanding as we have evolved. The ways in which we have managed to disseminate information on a mass scale for the last century and a half evidence the power of media. The town crier: a type of media. The Pony Express: a form of media. Paul Revere's fateful ride, when he yelled, "The British are coming!" might have been a hashtag campaign if executed today. Humans have always found ways to relay mass messages. The speed and distance at which these messages travel are what have changed. As the media has become a more efficient, expedient, and accessible force, its value has ballooned beyond simply being the prevailing method of disseminating information for a society. Just as importantly, it has become an economic juggernaut for the structure of global capitalism to generate wealth off our body shame—what I like to call the global Body-Shame Profit Complex (BSPC).

The earliest connection between information dissemination and revenue generation can be traced back to the first newspaper advertisement, which appeared in the *Boston News-Letter* in 1704. By the early 1900s, advertising had become its own industry and the primary source of revenue for countless newspapers.[16] Selling us things became a big deal. The arrival of radio and television exploded the possibilities of mass communication and ushered in an inexhaustible stream of potential revenue. According to statista.com, which tracks global advertising spending, the worldwide advertising industry spent $543.17 billion in 2018 to sell us pickles, rugs, brakes, beer, weight loss supplements, antiaging creams, skin lighteners, muscle supplements, plastic surgery, and tens of thousands of other completely useful and completely useless products and services.[17] We can be certain the advertisers who are spending more than half a trillion dollars per year to convince us to buy stuff are undoubtedly successful at their jobs and earning considerable profit from their efforts. However, let us not forget that advertisers are merely middlemen. They are being paid to sell industry products. If advertisers are reaping a financial boon, then the product makers are sipping Chandon from the starboard side of a yacht named the SS *Sucks to Be You*! Who are these product makers chugging pricey prosecco? A portion of them are the profiteers of the BSPC. Earnings for the global beauty market reached an epic $532 billion in 2019, and are projected to continue trending higher.[18] Whether we are buying hair dye to cover the grays or concealer to cover the blemishes, the beauty sector is grossing nearly as much money as the entire advertising industry spends, all to beneficently help us have . . . ahem . . . shinier hair, fewer wrinkles, and longer lashes! Sounds like poodle-science marketing to me. To offer some perspective, $532 billion is more than the gross domestic product of 170 nations (a disparity that has only grown larger since the first edition of this book).[19] What does this mean? Well, it means we are collectively spending more on lipstick, shampoo, and tanning spray than the entire economic infrastructure of three-fourths of the planet's countries. It also means if we all stopped buying beauty supplies, let's say . . . tomorrow, we would not only collapse the BSPC; we would tank the global economy. My hunch is that unlike the banks, we would not get a bailout!

Unapologetic Inquiry #13

How has body shame fueled your consumerism? What do you buy to "be normal," "fit in," or "fix your flaws"?

Our exploration into advertising and media is at its root a critique of the exploitative nature of capitalism and consumerism. Our economic systems shape how we see our bodies and the bodies of others, and they ultimately inform what we are compelled to do and buy based on that reflection. Profit-greedy industries work with media outlets to offer us a distorted perception of ourselves and then use that distorted self-image to sell us remedies for the distortion. Consider that the female body type portrayed in advertising as the ideal is possessed naturally by only 5 percent of American women. Whereas the average U.S. woman is five feet four inches tall and weighs 140 pounds, the average U.S. model is five feet eleven and weighs 117. Now consider a *People* magazine survey which reported that 80 percent of women respondents said images of women on television and in the movies made them feel insecure. Together, those statistics and those survey results illustrate a regenerative market of people who feel deficient based on the images they encounter every day, seemingly perfectly matched with advertisers and manufacturers who have just the products to sell them (us) to fix those imagined deficiencies.[20]

Buying to Be "Enough"

A 2017 article from *Self* magazine reported that the average American woman spends $15,000 on beauty products over the course of her lifetime. Nearly $3,000 is spent on mascara, $2,000 on eye shadow, and $1,700 on lipstick.[21] That, my friend, is an epic amount of lipstick. If I handed you $15,000 to read this book (I *really* want folks to read this book), what would you do with it? Let me make some guesses. Pay down debt? Put a down payment on a house? Take a vacation to some exotic location? Help your children or loved ones? Go back to school? Buy an alpaca? Whether I guessed your specific answer correctly or not, I am willing to bet five million of Bill Gates's dollars that you did not say, "Sonya, I would buy a lifetime supply of antiaging cream!" I have posed this question to thousands of people across the United States and abroad, and not one person has ever replied by telling me they'd buy a lifetime supply of hair dye, liposuction, weight loss or muscle-enhancing pills. No one has even said they would buy a sixty-year membership to their local SoulCycle gym. When given the opportunity to think about how we would spend our money if we thought of it as a powerful and abundant resource (which, by the way, it totally is), we choose things that bring us closest to the epicenter of our joy and remind us of what is central about being alive. In the depth of our hearts, we know that the answers have never been liposuction, gray-hair remedies, or the loss of twenty pounds, because in the grand scheme of a life well lived, eye liner, dress sizes, and ripped abs really don't matter.

We humans are masters of distraction, using makeup, weight loss, and a finely curated self-image to avoid being present to our fears, even as they build blockades around our most potent desires. Reading a bunker's worth of blemish-cream reviews is the perfect antidote if you want to keep avoiding those annoying university applications sitting on your desk—the ones you have yet to fill out even though you promised yourself you would go back to school. Fretting about the fifteen pounds you have been fretting about for fifteen years is a lighter load than paying down the $15,000 in credit card debt so you can finally start that business you always wanted. We are not "bad" or frivolous people for buying beauty products. Nor am I proposing that lipstick or any other such purchase is innately evil. Personally, I love a good MAC shade. (Film Noir is poppin'!)[22] I am proposing that reflecting on our purchases gives us an opportunity to investigate whether we are in alignment with our own unapologetic truth. Are we being manipulated by capitalism and the BSPC? If so, how we can take our power back?

> ### Radical Reflection
> *Our relationship with our money often mirrors our relationships with our bodies. When my relationship with me moves from a fear-based, lack-based, deficit-based relationship into a courageous, abundant, radical self-love relationship, intimate possibilities, financial possibilities, and creative possibilities unfold. Every single time!*

> ### Unapologetic Inquiry #14
> *When was the last time you made a purchase because you didn't feel "good enough"? Did the purchase change how you felt? If so, how and for how long?*

Best-Interest Buying vs. Detriment Buying

Divesting from the BSPC requires us to imagine what a radical self-love economy might look like. Manifesting such an economy entails observing our personal impact in the worldwide marketplace and asking ourselves, "What kind of consumer am I?" I propose that most of our purchases generally fall into two primary categories: best-interest buying and detriment buying. Best-interest buying is a model that asks us to allow our economic investments, whether they be lattes, lipsticks, neckties, or stock portfolios, to reflect our commitment to radical self-love for our own lives and for the lives of others. Best-interest buying furthers our radical self-love journey by connecting how we spend our resources with what we deeply want for our lives, not simply in the short term to avoid feelings of not being "enough." In this model, we ask ourselves if what we are buying is a desire rooted in radical self-love. Being a best-interest buyer does not happen overnight and is not a zero-sum proposition. Given how rarely we are in control of how products are sourced and made, it is easy to make purchases that pass muster in regard to our personal motives for buying them while subsequently being a source of harm because of exploitative or unethical practices at the hands of the product makers. These systems of oppression are intricately woven together and will be hard to fully divest from. When we are unable to do no harm, our work is to do as little harm as possible. We do not become best-interest buyers by being judgmental jerks toward ourselves about our purchases or flagellating ourselves for being suckers conned by the BSPC. Instead we continue gently asking ourselves about our motives, intentions, and impact. Radical self-love calls us toward a deeper investigation: "Why am I compelled to spend $180 on wrinkle-defying serum?" "Who or what may have been harmed in the making of this shirt?" Posing these questions to ourselves is likely a more effective and loving strategy than haranguing ourselves for making said purchases.

The act of inquiry serves as a lighthouse on our journey, there to help us locate our position in the wild seas of media and BSPC manipulation.

This does not mean we should be full-stop averse to changing our bodies, or that making makeup, fashion, or aesthetic choices is antithetical to radical self-love. What each of us needs to live in the fullness of our personal expression will be as varied as our individual bodies and dependent on our lived experiences. For example, when I have asked transgender people what they would do with $15,000, many have said they would spend it on gender-affirmation surgery (surgical procedures that change one's body to conform to one's gender identity).[23] This answer is unsurprising and completely aligned with radical self-love, which is about abiding in our most authentic selves. As we seek to do this, we are guided to move toward the most honest representation of our being. For some of us, moving away from body hyperconsciousness is key to that journey. For others, whose identities and bodies are more profoundly policed and erased by society, the desire to have those identities seen and affirmed is an essential aspect of the radical self-love journey. *Of course*, we can wear makeup, join a gym, and color our hair. I am a loud proponent of being unapologetically adorned. But the practice of inquiry shows us where we have adopted the media indoctrination that connects our worth and value to our appearance and external selves. That is what I call detriment buying.

We know we are on the island of detriment buying when our honest inquiries about why we made a purchase show us that our

> **Radical Reflection**
>
> *Although our actions are important, we learn more about ourselves when we examine our motives. Radical self-love inquiry is less about judging ourselves for "what" we do and far more about compassionately asking ourselves "why?"*

motivations were more intricately connected to our beliefs that we are somehow deficient or unworthy. Detriment buying leaves us feeling numbed out and disconnected from our bodies and our world. A great way to distinguish detriment buying from best-interest buying is to ask yourself, "Do I truly know I am no less worthy without these purchases? Am I buying this because it is an addition to the fullness of my already divine existence? Or is this purchase an effort to fix some presumed flaw? And if I think I am flawed, where is that message coming from? Who told me? Why do I believe them?" Our answers to these simple questions are a portal into a new way of being in relationship with ourselves, our bodies, and our money. Of course, this is not new at all; it is just our return to radical self-love!

Unapologetic Inquiry #15

One way to check if our desires for bodily change are motivated by authentic self-expression or shame is to ask ourselves, "Am I changing my body in ways that an oppressive body-shame system will reward me for?"

A Government for, by, and about Bodies

We cannot talk about bodies without talking about the systems that govern our bodies. If you are reading this book, you are probably located in some society with a government. That is, of course, unless you somehow found a copy of this book in a dark cave in a secret land where only you live, in which case ignore this section and consider yourself incredibly lucky! The rest of us live under systems of government that are, by their very nature, about rules, laws, and bodies. Allocation of resources, attribution of rights, and assignment of responsibilities in a society are all functions of governance, and they impact the daily lives of the governed (all of whom just happen to be people with bodies). Our systems and structures do not exist in a vacuum. These systems in many ways mirror the societies that made them. They are created and upheld by humans who have the same indoctrinations, beliefs, and shames that we all have. Those who govern are not immune to the inheritance of body shame, either as recipients or perpetrators. Our leaders mold and uphold systems of government that directly affect our experiences of body shame and body-based oppression. Officials use these positions of power to codify beliefs that are already present in their lives, in the lives of their constituents, and in society at large. The power to create laws also endows governments with the power to influence which bodies we accept as normal and which we do not, all through the validation of legality. To varying degrees and without very much thought, many of us have accepted what we have been told about our bodies and the bodies

> **Radical Reflection**
> *Systems of oppression stand or fall based on whether humans uphold or resist them. "We the people" have the power to uphold or resist body-based oppression.*

of others based on what our government allows, sanctions, ignores, or criminalizes. As governments wield authority and oversee systems, they are in a unique position to shape how we validate and stratify different bodies. Ultimately, they are responsible for creating laws and entities that either protect bodies or oppress them. Unfortunately, the history of government using its vast influence to ensure that all bodies are treated equitably has been about as consistent as a game of Russian roulette.

Did you know the following?

- Seventy-two countries have laws criminalizing homosexuality. In at least six countries, the death penalty can be applied to those found to be gay.[24]

- Immigrants can be deported from New Zealand for having a BMI (body mass index) over 35.[25]
- From the mid-seventeenth century until the 1970s many U.S. municipalities had city ordinances known as "Ugly Laws" which forbade visibly disabled people from accessing public spaces as they were deemed unsightly and inappropriate for public view.[26]
- The Asexualization Act of 1909 made it legal in California to forcibly sterilize anyone the state deemed "mentally ill," "mentally deficient," or possessing a "feeblemindedness." California was still forcibly sterilizing female prison inmates as recently as 2010. Most were inmates of color.[27]
- In Malta, if a kidnapper, "after abducting a person, shall marry such person, he shall not be liable to prosecution."[28]
- In Greece, a 2012 measure allows police to "detain people suspected of being HIV positive and force them to be tested." The measure also urges landlords to evict tenants who are HIV positive (to counter a perceived "public health threat").[29]

Legislating body shame is not a draconian practice of centuries bygone. The above laws are modern-day examples of how our governments build body-based oppression into everyday lives, codifying inequity and injustice for all types of bodies. From LGBTQIAA+ bodies to fat bodies, to disabled bodies and women's bodies, we live under systems that force us to judge, devalue, and discriminate against the bodies of others. Why, you might wonder, have we been so committed to discriminating against various bodies? To answer this question, we must look at the central currency of government: power.

The Center for American Women and Politics reports that forty-four women have held a U.S. governorship since the first woman was elected as a governor in 1925.[30] By contrast, the United States has had over twenty-three hundred male governors in its history.[31] Globally, women hold only 23 percent of the total available seats in national parliaments.[32] Consider that women represent approximately half the human population, and it becomes glaringly clear that this disparity is the manifestation of gender inequity. Right now, your favorite men's rights activist is yelling, "These feminists are so dumb! Duh, there are fewer women because women just don't get involved in politics as much as men do." My contemplative reply might be, "Hmm . . . I wonder how much the 144 years American women went without voting rights impacted that?" Even today in many countries, women must battle laws forbidding or obstructing their involvement in government. Even without the presence of such laws, women's involvement in the political landscape cannot be separated from the scrutiny, objectification, and sexism they still face while running for office. All over the world women must traverse a hostile terrain that questions female suitability for political service while excusing gender discrimination by using outdated, disparaging tropes about female intelligence, ability, and acumen as justification for that bias. Naomi Wolf, journalist and author of *The Beauty Myth*, writes, "A culture fixated on female thinness is not an obsession about female beauty but an obsession about female obedience. Dieting is the most potent political sedative in history. A quietly mad population is a tractable one."[33]

Wolf strategically illustrates how body-shame social messaging is used as a means of controlling and centralizing political power. We need look no further than the 2016 U.S. presidential election to see Wolf's thesis in action. Candidate Hillary Clinton was exhaustingly scrutinized about her aesthetic presentation. Outfits, makeup, hairstyles were all fodder for the twenty-four-hour news cycle. Even the pro-Hillary, hundred-thousand-plus-member Facebook group Pantsuit Nation chose her penchant for eschewing skirts and dresses as the name of their collective, inadvertently directing public focus to her physical appearance rather than her decades of political experience.

At every corner, women's political access hinges on society's ability to see them in alignment with the default ideals of women first and then politicians. But political gatekeeping based on bodies exists beyond the realm of sex and gender binaries. In workshops, I often ask participants to consider the forty-four women who have been governors throughout the country's history and to take guesses at what those numbers might be if we were to break them down by various identities. How many people of color have been governor? What about the number of openly gay or lesbian people? How about people with disabilities? Or transgender folks? Undoubtedly people begin to see how those numbers winnow down to fewer and fewer diverse bodies being represented in our "representative" government. But we do not have to guess. The numbers speak for themselves:

- Twenty-six governors have been people of color.[34]
- Six governors have been disabled.[35]
- Two governors have been openly gay or lesbian.[36]
- Zero have been openly transgender.

Remember, most of us live at the intersection of gender, age, race, disability, and so on, our identities overlapping. Which means representation is nearly nonexistent for bodies living at the axis of multiple identities. The United States has had only one woman of color serve as governor and one lesbian woman. All the other intersections of identity . . . zero. This country is not an anomaly in its history of centralizing political power toward a specific sort of body; most nations have a default body in their government structures. Although social and cultural realities may shift what those bodies look like, using default bodies to establish a social hierarchy and distribute power and resources is a global phenomenon. The statistics above illustrate an irrefutable truth: body shame and oppression are both symptoms of and tools in a far more complex and sweeping system of access and resources. A system that impacts not only how we feel about ourselves but also our opportunities and ability to thrive in the world. There is a reason we hate our bodies, and it isn't because of Curtis, our mamas, or even our low self-esteem. We are saddled with body shame because it is an age-old system whose roots and pockets are deep. Body shame flourishes in our world because profit and power depend on it.

Unapologetic Inquiry #16

How does body shame impact political power? How has body shame made you less powerful?

Call It What It Is: Body Terrorism

At the beginning of the book I described how the containers of self-esteem and self-confidence simply cannot hold the breadth and depth of radical self-love. As humans, we're in need of a radical love to transform how our world deals with bodies. I hope by this point in the book I've made my case. Our work must be radical if we are to combat the consistent inundation of toxic media messages, laws, and regulations seeping body shame and body-based oppression into every aspect of our society. Inequity in our government systems, manipulation in our media—no matter the structure under examination, ultimately each of us bears the personal, social, and political burden of a widespread and deeply troubling relationship with bodies. The results of this reality are nothing short of devastating. Gross inequality and disenfranchisement across social experiences, poor public-health outcomes, and unjust legislation are systemic representations of centuries of infusing body shame into every sector of public and private life. A National Center for Health

Statistics report (as recounted in the *New York Times*) indicated that suicide rates in 2014 were the highest they had been in thirty years. Native Americans, a community whose bodies have been met with an interminable history of oppression, erasure, and inequity, saw the highest rise in rates, with a horrifying increase of 89 percent.[37] A ProPublica analysis of federal data regarding police-involved shootings found that young Black men between ages fifteen and nineteen were twenty-one times more likely to be killed by the police than young White men of the same age.[38] By the first half of 2017, the Human Rights Campaign had tracked the rise of over 115 pieces of new anti-LGBTQIAA+ legislation across the United States.[39] These numbers tell a story about how our societies fare under the pressures of body-based oppressions.

Entire communities are dying from epidemic levels of suicide. Parents around the country are immobilized with the fear that a routine traffic stop might result in the indiscriminate murder of their child at the hands of a police officer. (This fear is so commonplace that thousands of Black parents find themselves having "the talk" with their kids: a detailed discussion of what their children should

> ### Radical Reflection
> *Our beliefs about bodies disproportionately impact those whose race, gender, sexual orientation, ability, and age deviate from our default notions. The further from the default, the greater the impact. We are all affected—but not equally.*

do if the police stop them, in the hope that they might prepare them with enough information to arrive home safe each night.) No sooner than gay and lesbian people celebrate the landmark legislative win of being able to legally marry the person they love, they are forced to watch state after state sanction their continued discrimination in restaurants, in medical facilities, and on the job. Our world is disconnected from the site of these inequities. We look at statistics and see policy and laws, forgetting how they are created by and enacted on our bodies. Across gender, sexual orientation, race, size, age, and ability level, our systems are constantly affirming or denouncing bodies, communicating to us what we should and should not consider valid about other people's bodies while simultaneously detailing for us what we should and should not accept about our own.

On December 28, 2014, seventeen-year-old trans youth Leelah Alcorn intentionally stepped into highway traffic and was hit by an eighteen-wheeled truck. In her suicide note, Leelah detailed her family's rejection of her trans identity and their refusal to give her permission to receive gender-affirming surgery.[40] It is tempting to see Leelah's story as the individual allegory of a highly religious family's dogma and its tragic impact on a teen. But to allow the analysis to stop there would be to miss the myriad ways in which systems much bigger than Leelah's family failed to protect her. Leelah's story indicts our entire society for its unwillingness to care for all bodies, thus making it virtually impossible for some of us to live lives of radical self-love—or even to continue wanting to live at all. A lack of school-based resources able to address the needs of trans students, inaccessible mental health supports, a society that demands that bodies conform to rigid gender assignments: these larger systemic realities contributed as much to Leelah's heartrending death as her family's bigotries. A long line of people and systems blocked Leelah's vision of a rich and authentic future for herself. That obstruction ended in her death.

Unapologetic Inquiry #17

If you could share something with Leelah that would have given her hope, what would you have said? Write it down. Share it with yourself on the days you are struggling to find hope.

Living with mounting evidence that society at every turn will reject our attempts to exist unapologetically in our bodies is to live in a state of terror. Dragging ourselves through a lifetime of self-hate endorsed and encouraged by our media and our political and economic systems is a terrifying way to live, and yet millions of people exist in this constant state of fear every day. It is an act of terrorism against our bodies to perpetuate body shame and to support body-based oppression. I call this "body terrorism."

Terrorism is defined as "the systematic use of terror especially as a means of coercion."[41] It takes no more than a brief review of the historic and present-day examples of media manipulation and legislative oppression to acknowledge that we are indeed being coerced into body shame for both economic and political reasons. When using the term *body terrorism*, I have been met with resistance and accused of hyperbole. "You are being dismissive of the danger of 'real' terrorism," detractors have said. This knee-jerk response to our understanding of terrorism is shaped by a public discourse that continues to separate the fear and violence we navigate every day in our bodies from the more overtly political violence we see happening around the world. We must not minimize or negate the impact of being told to hate or fear our bodies and the bodies of others. Living in a society structured to profit from our self-hate creates a dynamic in which we are so terrified of being ourselves that we adopt terror-based ways of being in our bodies. All this is fueled by a system that makes large quantities of money off our shame and bias. These experiences are not divergent but complementary.

On the morning of the presidential inauguration of Donald Trump, I was leaving Washington, D.C., after hosting an event called the Peace Ball the night before. When I arrived at the airport and proceeded through the body scanner, I was stopped for additional screening. Apparently, my groin area had signaled the machine's alert system, and I was going to be subjected to a pat down. This was not my first time navigating TSA screening procedures. I am, after all, a fat Black woman with the word *radical* in her job title on her business cards. The TSA agent rubbed her hands up my inner thigh and without warning rubbed my vulva. My response was involuntary. "Why are you touching my vagina?" I blurted out loud enough for the entire security line to hear. Confounded by my outburst, the TSA agent quickly called for her supervisor, who demanded that I be taken to a private screening room where I would be less disruptive as the agents groped my genitalia. Powerless, I wept silently as the agent completed the pat down, and then I exited the private room, shaken by a deep sense of violation. I had been sexually assaulted—simply in order to be able to carry on to my next destination, under the orders of the government, and paid for by my tax dollars.

The next day, anxiety hijacked me as I walked into a different airport while headed home from my travels. Initially I couldn't locate the source of the anxiety buzzing through my chest and legs, and then I recalled the events of the day before: I was having a trauma response. My body had cataloged yesterday's incident as a traumatic violation and was bracing in terror for the experience to happen again. Later, I learned from several transgender friends that the TSA scanners are designed to alert agents to "anomalies" in the groin area. Specifically, agents are instructed to additionally screen all people whose groins appear to differ from their perceived gender. Across the country, large numbers of transgender people are also being forced to navigate similar invasive sexual traumas simply to board a plane. We are told that the procedures of the TSA are supposed to make us safer. I did not feel safe. I was terrified and without recourse. While I stood in the private screening room with tears rolling down my face, the least of my concerns was some random person living out a political vendetta against the United States during my flight. I was terrified of having my genitalia touched without my consent by a stranger as a requisite for passage to my next destination. This is body terrorism. Believing that it is preferable to walk into the path of an eighteen-wheeler than to live another day being rejected by the whole of society is a belief rooted firmly in the soil of being subjected to body terrorism.

Unapologetic Inquiry #18

Can you recall an incident when you felt a sense of terror about being in your body? What did you do to navigate the feeling?

The historical and contemporary violence associated with body hatred is widespread and horrific. We cannot continue to normalize these actions as simply inconvenient or unfortunate. The outcomes of body terrorism are deadly. From violence against people of color (e.g., lynching, slavery, the Holocaust, internment camps); to LG-BTQIAA+ bodies being regularly assaulted, murdered, and driven to suicide; to rape and sexual assault; to the bombing of abortion clinics and the murder of physicians based on people's rights to autonomy over their own bodies; to the involuntary sterilization of people with disabilities; to the debilitating shame that people around the world live with as a result of the psychological attacks our social and media machines wage against us (ending in bulimia, anorexia, addiction, stigma, racism, homophobia, ableism, sizeism, ageism, transphobia, mass self-hatred, and senseless violence)—it is clear that there is nothing rhetorical or hyperbolic about detailing the impacts of body hatred and calling the promotion of such hatred on any scale an act of body-based terrorism.[42]

The framework of radical self-love seeks to engage people in the process of individual transformation. But as importantly, it seeks to dismantle the structural and systemic emotional, psychological, and physical violence meted out against "different" bodies all over the planet. Those who profit from our self-hatred are well served to minimize its impact and disconnect it from the larger social framework of violence and intimidation that allows oppression and injustice to thrive. Discrimination, social inequality, and injustice are manifestations of our inability to make peace with the body: our own and others'. By making these connections we build the foundation to foster a world of radical, unapologetic self-love, which translates to radical human action in the service of a more just, equitable, and compassionate world.

Radical Reflection

Take a moment to consider how body terrorism has impacted your life and the lives of people you love. Imagine what might be possible in a world without it.

3

Building a Radical Self-Love Practice in an Age of Loathing

Mapping Our Way out of Shame and into Radical Self-Love

Recall from Chapter 1 my discussion of the Three Peaces, which we must reckon with if we want to abandon the body-shame army and commence our radical self-love assignment. To recap, kicking body shame in the butt means we must be willing to do the following:

1. Make peace with not understanding.
2. Make peace with difference.
3. Make peace with our bodies.

Well, my friend, we have arrived on the shores of the final P. Up to this point, we have unpacked the difference between self-confidence and radical self-love. We have learned why self-love must be a radical act if we want a transformed world. We've revisited the ick and discomfort of our body-shame origins, disrobed the media and the Body-Shame Profit Complex, explored the role of government in shaping rights and laws that privilege some bodies while punishing others. We have examined the traumatizing and fatal outcomes of living under a system of body terrorism. If you are currently considering a permanent relocation to that autonomous cave without a government that I mentioned earlier, I want you to know that I do not blame you. Radical self-love can feel like an impossibility when observed beside the deluge of body shame we see crashing all around us. What I also want you to know is that *radical self-love is not an impossibility.* It is not even a destination. *It is your inherent sense of self.* You came here, to this planet, as unapologetic radical love. Body terrorism depends on your amnesia for its survival. Our singular focus in this chapter is to help you practice the third Peace. Making peace with your body is not about finding some obscure pathway to the peninsula of "liking my thighs." Making peace with your body is about awakening to who you have always been: the physical, spiritual, and energetic manifestation of radical self-love. Together, we will disrupt decades of tired body-shame practices using the only map we ever needed for this journey: a map back to ourselves.

Body terrorism is a hideous tower whose primary support beam is the belief that there is a hierarchy of bodies. We uphold the system by internalizing this hierarchy and using it to situate our own value and worth in the world. When our personal value is dependent on the lesser value of other bodies, radical self-love is unachievable. By this point, my hope is that you can see how you and millions of others have been manipulated into a system of body shame. More importantly, I want you to know that this system is destructible, and the fastest way to obliterate its control over us is to do the scary work of tearing down those pillars of hierarchy inside ourselves. At the same time, we must trust

> ### Radical Reflection
> *Theodore Roosevelt is frequently quoted as saying, "Comparison is the thief of joy." I'm not sure if he said it, but the sentiment was totally right! Go get your joy back!*

that what will be left standing is our own divine enoughness, absent of any need for comparison.

Living a radical self-love life is a process of de-indoctrination. It demands that we look unflinchingly at our current set of beliefs about ourselves and the world and get willing to explore them. I call this the act of being fear-facing. Fear-facingness is not the absence of fear but the interrogation of it. While agonizing over the completion of this book, I spent some time emptying my brain at a friend's home on a private beach in Long Island, Bahamas. The island was slow and kind, like a good grandfather. During one of our excursions we drove westward, down miles of crumbled, unforgiving asphalt, until we arrived at a small beach. The sign at the edge of the road read, "Warning. Dean's Hole is the deepest in the world. Swim at Your Own Risk." Two feet from the beach shore the cerulean water stops being waist high, and within a few steps the ocean floor drops into a cavernous 663-feet-deep hole. Despite my being a competent swimmer, fear consumed me. I was certain that the mouth of the deep blue hole would suck me down to its watery floor. In my research, I would later discover that my fear mirrored the exact superstitions that keep native islanders away from the hole. Needless to say, I kept my distance.

It was at Dean's Hole where I met Davide Carrera, a free-diving champion from Italy. Free diving entails using a cable to descend into extreme ocean depths without the use of breathing equipment. Davide holds his country's record with a 111-meter dive (yes, that is the equivalent of diving off a thirty-five-story building)![1] He was taking a break from competition and enjoying the beach with his fellow divers when we struck up a conversation. (It is in these chance encounters that I am reminded that if we are open to it, we will find confirmation of our divine pathway all around us.) "The dive is a spiritual thing," Davide said. "I learn how to listen to my body. I must listen or I will die. In the water, I must learn the difference between fear and danger." He did not know it, but Davide was describing the journey of radical self-love. It is damn scary to probe the depths of the thoughts, ideas, and subconscious principles governing our daily lives. To be fear-facing is to learn the distinction between fear and danger. It is to look directly at the source of the fear and assess if we are truly in peril or if we are simply afraid of the unknown. The unknown is like fog, and, of course, fog is frightening. Who knows what obstructions could be lurking about? What if there is a deer soon to be splayed on my windshield? What if I careen off a cliff while driving in the thick soup of fog? Living with body shame and body terrorism is to be stuck in an endless "what if" fog: a place of inertia. The only way out of the fog is through it. We must dive into the unknown, trusting that our bodies will help us discern fear from danger. There is always a clearing on the other side of the fog. To be fear-facing is to navigate cautiously and with alertness but to continue our journey. Before we parted, I asked Davide what continues to call him to the sport of free diving. He beamed at me, the Bahamian sun lucent behind him, and said, "Every meter is a tiny freedom." Yes, it is. So let's dive in!

Unapologetic Inquiry #19

In what ways has the fog of living in body shame hindered your most amazing life? What is incomplete, unexplored, ignored inside you because of your belief that something about you and your body is wrong?

Thinking, Being, Doing

You can't self-help your way back to radical self-love. Reading this book will not be enough to get you there because radical self-love is a return to the love of our whole being. It requires a whole-being approach to our lives and bodies. Living a radical self-love life is a process of:

- Thinking
- Doing
- Being

Have you ever spent time with your thoughts? Whew, talk about a scene from some dark, dystopic horror film. Our thoughts are an amalgamation of all manner of input mixed with just a dash of original content. Often it's a mess in there, a vessel filled with self-loathing and judgment. It's unsurprising that we avoid being present with our thoughts. We think tons of repugnant, petrifying, miserable things about our own bodies and other folks' bodies every single day. It's easy to slip into a pit of shame for having these thoughts. Unfortunately, the sense of shame keeps us distant and detached from our personal center of governance. It puts us out of operational control. Have you ever felt like you were living your life on autopilot? Somehow you just keep recycling old behaviors and ideas that you know do not serve you, but you can't seem to interrupt them. You are not alone! That sense of autopilot is the result of being disconnected from our thoughts. Without our awareness, thoughts run covert operations all through our lives, assassinating our sense of worth and blowing up our connections with other humans. When we avoid our thoughts, they go rogue. Awareness of our thoughts highlights the how and why of our behaviors. It gives us a fighting chance at transforming how we live in the world.

"But how do I break out of the fear of exploring the catacombs of my thoughts?" Great question! Answer: *You are not your thoughts!* Our thoughts are a hybrid of information forged from our own experiences, traumas, successes, failures, and massive input from our external world. All those media messages about good bodies and default bodies: they're in your thoughts. All the government-endorsed ideas of safe bodies and dangerous bodies: they're in your thoughts. You have been given thoughts, and just like that shame sweater, you do not have to keep them.

On a flight to Morocco several years ago, I was convinced that the all-Arab, all-male flight-attendant crew were terrorists preparing to hijack the plane. What a horrible thought! I felt awful for the judgments and irrational fear I was having about these men based on their bodies. But the truth is I didn't give myself those thoughts. A 2012 article on the website of the Society of Personality and Social Psychology reviewed multiple studies and found that "people exposed to Arabs-as-terrorists media may be more likely to perceive a seemingly neutral interaction with an Arab as threatening or aggressive, thereby influencing the course of the interaction."[2] Constant visual images of Arab men hijacking planes and buses and kidnapping Americans had been poured into my psyche for almost twenty years. Consciously, I knew that those images I saw on television were not a representation of all or even most Arab men. I knew that the U.S. "war on terror" was causing grave harm to Arab and Muslim people around the world. It did not matter that the statistical likelihood of my plane being hijacked by twelve incredibly attractive, uniformed flight attendants was beyond negligible. Per a Cato Institute analysis, my chances of dying in an attack committed by a foreign-born terrorist were 1 in 3.6 million—a.k.a. not highly likely.[3]

Despite all my information, the thoughts were still there. But because I have practiced being aware of my thoughts, I could identify how the thoughts were mine—as in, happening inside my brain—but they were not me. They were part of a bounty of ideas and messages I had received from multiple sources that had subcon-

> **Radical Reflection**
>
> *Say it again, for the folks in the bleachers: You are not your thoughts! That said, avoiding your thoughts will not help you train your brain to think new ones.*
> *You must look at them with gentle kindness and say, "Thank you for sharing." And, with love, release them.*

sciously penetrated my psyche. My ability to notice the thoughts and distinguish them from my own authentic ideas helped me source where they were coming from. Those thoughts were not me, and I had a choice about whether to challenge or act on them or not.

Unapologetic Inquiry #20

Can you recall a time when you had a body-shaming thought about someone else's body? Can you identify where some of those ideas came from?

Being intimately connected to our thoughts is not enough to change our behaviors. Knowing why we do something will not necessarily keep us from doing it. Doing is a choice. It is an act of will. Doing often demands that we act despite our thoughts. When we are no longer on autopilot, we are forced to deal with the discomfort of new action. Think of radical self-love as resistance training against our decades-old, tight, calcified thoughts. Adopting actions that promote radical self-love is comparable to working a muscle that has not been moved in years. It's going to be sore and tender. You are going to be tired. But the exhaustion and frustration will lessen over time, and there will be ease where there once was pain. Old habits of body-shaming yourself, judging the bodies of others under your breath, acting from a sense of failure or lack of self-worth will become uncomfortable behaviors, and radical self-love action will begin to feel like the path of least resistance. Over time, you will notice that your thoughts flow in alignment with your behaviors. The junk in your brain will start to occupy less space, and when it starts to reclutter your thoughts you will recognize it and move it out. You are thinking and acting in radical self-love.

Have you ever met someone and thought, "Wow, Mary just emanates love from her whole being"? The experience of being around someone who radiates a discernable energy is an act of being. Though it is not always a positive experience. We engage every day with people whose energy is not welcoming—sometimes even downright hostile—but we also meet people who radiate unencumbered love. Children are a glorious example of this ability to radiate love. Having not yet experienced layers of body shame, young kids are reflections of the source relationship of all our beings: love.

> **Radical Reflection**
> *Notice the next time your actions are not in alignment with your thoughts. The discomfort you feel is trying to tell you something. It is pushing you beyond just thinking or doing, toward radical self-love being.*

We, too, can access that source relationship. Through the power of thought and action we become who we have always been; we enter what feels like a new way of being in our bodies and in the world but is actually a return to our inherent state of being: radical self-love.

Four Pillars of Practice

We know that adopting a radical self-love lifestyle is a process of thinking, doing, and being. But changing the way we think, act, and are in our daily lives can feel like an assignment of planetary proportions. Implementing practices to structure this endeavor is the equivalent of turning on the high beams amid the fog. Rather than collapsing under an avalanche of new ideas and behaviors, we can install signposts and guardrails that help us know if we are still on the road to radical self-love. The four pillars of practice can help us corral our wily thinking, fortify love-laden action, and give us access to a new way of being in the world. The pillars are:

1. Taking out the toxic
2. Mind matters

3. Unapologetic action
4. Collective compassion

Dismantling body shame and body terrorism is a process of de-indoctrination requiring that we excavate the thoughts we have internalized about bodies and evict the voices of judgment, hierarchy, and shame. Remember when I recounted how my fear of sharing a selfie was an early prompt in my radical self-love journey? The voice I heard in my head telling me I was too fat, ugly, and Black to post the photo was not my voice. It was the propaganda of body shame, the "outside voice." Our inherent sense of radical self-love doesn't speak to us with cruelty or viciousness. Radical self-love does not malign our gender, sexuality, race, disability, weight, age, acne, scars, illnesses. A world of body terrorism that impugns us because of our identities is the only thing that would dare speak to us with such malice. Just as the Three Peaces offer us a framework for divesting from a lifetime of shame and judgment, the four pillars teach us to make peace with our bodies by distinguishing and diminishing the outside voice and cultivating a practice of listening more deeply to our authentic selves, our radical self-love voice, our "inside voice."

> **Radical Reflection**
>
> *I have always had a very loud voice. My mother would constantly admonish me for talking too loudly. "Use your inside voice!" she would say. Next time you hear someone speaking body shame over themselves, politely suggest that they use their "inside voice," and share what the phrase means.*

The first two pillars, taking out the toxic and mind matters, ask us to imagine the inside and outside voices as though they were volume knobs in our minds. These radical self-love practices teach us how to adjust the sound and filter the static, turning up our authentic voice and tuning out our body-shame brainwashing. Pillar 3, unapologetic action, integrates our thinking with our physical selves, moving our radical self-love practice out of our heads and into our bodies. Lastly, the pillar of collective compassion synthesizes how we emanate radical self-love, learning to radiate love through our own beings and onto the beings of others. One of the easiest ways to build out your daily practice is by grabbing a copy of the *Your Body Is Not an Apology Workbook* (due April 2021). The workbook is an activity and reflection-based guide designed to enable you to put these pillars into practice in your life. It is constructed to help you move from concept to action and allow you to try on the thinking, doing, being process, ultimately landing you in the seat of your most powerful location: reconnected to your inherent sense of radical self-love.

Pillar 1: Taking Out the Toxic

To live in a world of body terrorism is akin to forcibly imbibing gallons of body shame daily. From the moment we tune into television, radio, computer, or our phones in the morning until we close the laptop or put the phone on silent at night, we are inundated with messages relaying our supposed inherent deficiency. The average adult consumes fifteen and a half hours of media each day, and even when they don't contain overt body shame, the shows we watch, the music we listen to, and the articles we read deliver messages about bodies in the world, including our own.[4] Taking in toxic messages blocks our pathway to radical self-love without any real effort on our part. Just walking down the street or standing in the grocery store checkout line can be a stroll down body-shame lane thanks to billboards, bus advertisements, and tabloid covers. By engaging in the everyday activities of our society, we subconsciously absorb views about our bodies that are antithetical to radical self-love. Therefore, being connected to our thoughts is a crucial process for battling body shame.

Marketers diversify their body-terrorism tactics with both conscious and subconscious directives. There is nothing subconscious about "Don't delay! Lose that unsightly belly flab now!" Advertisements like this are designed for immediacy, urging you to act now because your body is awful!

Unapologetic Inquiry #21

What was your last body-shame impulse purchase? Can you recall what thoughts moved you to make the purchase?

Equally sinister are the advertisements that remind us by repetition and erasure that unless we are youthful, blonde, thin, able-bodied, and muscular, with perfectly white teeth and glossy hair, we are fatally flawed and will need their product . . . eventually. (By the way, *no one* is all those things forever.) Advertisers and product makers want your money now. Are they willing to wait until you have watched sixty hours of television actors with perfect gleaming teeth and have finally awakened to the epiphany that you must buy teeth-whitening strips? Of course! But why bother waiting? Body-Shame Profit Complex profiteers know it is easier and more economically efficient to sell us body shame directly, to simply say "You suck" rather than allude to it. They prefer to highlight your epic flaws in grand detail on repeat until you get up off your couch and go give them your money!

Not only does this toxic messaging impact our spending, turning us into detriment buyers, but it also impacts how we talk about ourselves and others. Let's say you are out shopping for new jeans, and as you begin to try them on you think aloud, "I have to get rid of this unsightly belly flab!" You know you have never used the words *unsightly* and *flab* together, but suddenly you are a parrot for body-shame advertisers, speaking their carefully crafted messages over your own body. Toxic messages become our internal outside voice. After we've ingested enough body shame, these declarations become the narrative through which we speak about our own bodies, often without even noticing.

What can we do to get out of the toxic sludge of media marketing? Limit our media intake. If we cannot limit it, be intentional about what we ingest. Next time you are watching television, notice what commercials your favorite shows air between scenes. Those commercials indicate what advertisers believe about you as a consumer. Commercials use racial and gender stereotypes to target your wallets because they know that doing so works. This is a perfect place to put best-interest buying into practice. Television shows make money through ratings and advertising. Each show you watch puts money in some producer's and advertiser's pockets. Ask yourself, "Do this show and its commercials align with my radical self-love values?" If the answer is no, then the next question is "Why am I giving them my money?" If we think of our time and brain capacity as dollars, we may become a bit more particular about how we spend them. Are you following social media influencers with millions of followers and selfies that could double for *Vogue* covers? What about media personalities who target marginalized groups as scapegoats for social problems? Whether they are making you feel inadequate or offering up the projected inadequacies of others to make themselves feel more valuable, social media can be a cesspool of body shame and body terrorism. Only when we are connected to our thoughts can we identify how they are being dragged along by toxic media. If you have a body-shame hangover after you watch, read, or listen to something, it's time to take out the toxic.

Pillar 2: Mind Matters

If pillar 1 is the equivalent of a body-shame cleanse (far more satisfying than the juice version), then pillar 2 is a Marie Kondo purge where we empty out the attic and basement and consider what we might do with all the amazing space we've freed up. Once we have stopped imbibing body shame on a daily basis, we can begin to explore how our old ways of thinking have kept us stuck in cycles that dishonor our bodies. Body shame not only shapes how we see our bodies, it also clouds the lens through which we view our lives. If living a radical self-love life is a process of thinking, doing, and being, then "mind matters" asks us to try on some new mental attire. Let's call it the season's latest collection on the radical self-love runway.

Over the years, we have collected some crappy beliefs about our bodies. We've been taught that our bodies are entities to control and subjugate. We have treated our bodies like machines that are always on the fritz. In Eve Ensler's 2011 TED Talk "Suddenly My Body," she details how she spent most of her life disembodied, never considering her body a part of her being.[5] This remained true until she wrote *The Vagina Monologues* during a period in which she describes herself as becoming a "driven vagina." Still, her body was outside her. She saw it as a utensil, an instrument she used to get things done. It was when she got cancer that she realized her body was not an implement at her disposal but a part of her. Her body did not have cancer; she had cancer. Eve discovered that she and her body would have to integrate if she wanted to fight the disease that had attacked them both. They needed each other. The concept of "mind matters" asks us to reconsider our relationship with our bodies. How do we end the cold war with it and become allies in achieving our best lives? This pillar of practice is about reconciliation. In her poem "Three," Nayyirah Waheed captures the fullness of the second pillar in six perfect lines:

and i said to my body. softly.
'i want to be your friend.'
it took a long breath.

and replied
'i have been waiting my
whole life for this.'[6]

Guess what? Your brain is part of your body! Why am I yelling this?
Because too often we treat our brain as though it's a separate operating system tucked away in a room we call the skull. Our tendency to
divorce our brains from our bodies is one of the sneaky ways in
which body shame thrives. Isolating our brains gives us permission
to treat them differently. Depression, bipolar disorder, and other examples of neurodivergence[7] are stigmatized because we are unwill-
ing to extend the same care and treatment to our brains that we
afford our bodies. If I broke my arm and never went to a see a doctor,
not only would I be in extreme pain, but the people in my life would
be incensed by such a reckless choice. Yet we make statements like
"It's all in your head" all the time, minimizing the experiences of our
brains and neglecting their care.

Reintegrating our brains and
our bodies is a necessity for a radical self-love life. Pillar 2 highlights
how our reintegration gives us access to new levels of care and offers
us new opportunities to examine
our thought patterns and, with
hard work, create new ones. I may
never get rid of my clinical depression, but I can disentangle it from
body shame. Mind-matters tools like meditation and reframing
have helped me see my depression as another unique way my body
exists in the world rather than as a shame to avoid or hide.

> ### Radical Reflection
> *Phrases like "Get over it!"
> and "It's all in your head" are
> rooted in ableism. They are
> body terrorism against
> non-normative brains. Let's
> stop telling people to "get
> over it" and start asking,
> "How can I help you heal?"*

Expanding our mind's capacity for radical self-love means we
may need to tear down some mental walls. If radical self-love is an

open floor plan, expanding our space for connection and joy, rigidity and judgment are concrete walls, cutting off visibility and partitioning us off from our best lives. Pillar 2 is about expansive thinking, and expansive thinking is not possible unless we see our bodies and our lives with nuance. We are not either/or beings; we comprise a multitude of gray shades. Inviting love into our contradictions and uncertainties takes a wrecking ball to those concrete slabs of separation, giving us much more space to decorate with love.

Pillar 3: Unapologetic Action

If we are diligent in our practice of pillars 1 and 2, the volume of our external body shame can over time become a light buzz while our own resounding voice of radical self-love begins to ring loudly in our ears. There is no better time to get started on the "doing" portion of this work. Radical self-love is a muscle, and as with every other muscle, if we do not work it, atrophy will set in. Living in a world of body terrorism is like having our sense of value and innate worth set in a plaster cast for decades. Cracking open the cast and moving through the world in tune with our bodies can feel like working out our trapezius muscle. (What does that muscle even do?) There has never been a more perfect time to lean into the discomfort and fear. Remember, most of the fear is just fog.

It is difficult to deeply love a stranger. Familiarity breeds fondness. Pillar 3, unapologetic action, asks us to get to know these bodies of ours. If you have been avoiding looking at or touching your body, this is your chance to shift. By now, we understand our avoidance of being intimate with our bodies as part of being conditioned to believe that our bodies are bad, wrong, or disgusting. No one wants to hang out with a bad, wrong body. As we clear out those thoughts we are better able to see our bodies for what they truly are: amazing vessels, capable of awesome feelings, sensations, and experiences. By getting to know them, we open ourselves to deeper levels of pleasure, care, and ultimately radical love. Pillar 3 invites you to take yourself on a body expedition and discover your own remarkable landscape.

Not only have we avoided intimately knowing our bodies, we have forgotten that our bodies like doing stuff—walking, dancing, running, having sex! Body shame has severed our love of activity. In the chronicles of body shame, movement became a thing we avoided lest we jiggle while in motion! Unapologetic action is our departure from those old stories, prompting us to reconnect to the joys of movement. Many of us cannot recall a time when moving our bodies was something other than a way to punish them for failing to meet society's fictitious ideals. But just as we were once babies who loved our bodies, we were also babies who loved moving them. We can invite ourselves back to this place. There was magic there.

Pillar 3 is not singularly focused on our physical selves; it also summons us to new action by telling ourselves new stories. In Chapter 2, we discussed the characteristics of our early memories of body shame. We acknowledged how the things we were teased about or shamed for became part of how we saw ourselves later in life. Those early incidents became the yarn tethering our adult selves to our childhood histories of shame and isolation. Unapologetic action empowers us to make new stories, better than the ones we've been saddled with for years. Humans have made up stories since the beginning of time. Some of the stories have helped us understand this wild ride through humanity, whereas others have kept us cut off from radical self-love. We no longer must be bound by crappy stories. Humans made them up. You are human. Make a better story.

Pillar 4: Collective Compassion

In the beginning of my workshops, I tell participants that they can do everything I say, employ the Three Peaces in every area of their life, trace their body-shame origin story back to its inception, denounce the Body-Shame Profit Complex from the highest rooftop, and rock the first three pillars like nobody's business. But if they avoid pillar 4, collective compassion, then radical self-love will continue to elude them. Every word in this book is unsustainable without the fourth pillar. Collective compassion is the "being" part of radical self-love. It is our internal compass, quickly alerting us when we are off course. Not only does collective compassion provide an internal structure of governance (i.e., the rules that guide our personal work), it is also the bridge to the *socially* transformative power of radical self-love. Collective compassion guides us toward how we ought to treat ourselves, but as importantly, it is our directive for "being" with others.

Have you ever run into someone many years after the last time you saw them only to discover that they had undergone some phenomenal inner transformation? I am not talking about weight loss or a new haircut. I am talking a brand-new life. Perhaps they got sober after years of addiction. Maybe they healed a relationship that appeared completely irreparable from the outside. Whatever the transformation, when you saw them, you were flabbergasted. I am guessing your next thought was not, "Hey! I could totally do that!" For most humans, transformation does not seem achievable from the distant shores of another person's life. From far away, transformation looks like a miracle, or the result of magical powers possessed by the transformed person. Transformation is not magic. It's hard work. But it is also doable work. When we can see another person's labor toward their transformation, we know it is not some secret sauce but instead a daily commitment to a new way of life.

Up close we can also see that they are not doing the work alone! Transformation and healing demand that we open ourselves up to others. For many of us, this is the highest hurdle on the radical self-love road. Body shame and body terrorism have made us profoundly distrusting. We've been judged and mocked too many times. We have vowed to never subject ourselves to such hurt again. I want you to know I understand. But learning to trust others is indivisible from learning to trust yourself. You will need to practice both to get back to radical self-love. If you are working to rid yourself of years of body shame by being Clark Kent in a phone booth, I am sorry, love, but you will not come out as Superman. You are going to need someone to lean against while you pull up those tights. Truthfully, radical self-love is not the work of superheroes but of community and connection. Pillar 4 asks you to move beyond self-reliance to collective care. We must learn to *be* with each other if we plan to get free.

Before body shame stripped us of our inherent sense of self-worth, it stripped us of compassion. We saw failure in every mirror; we judged our every thought. We berated and abused ourselves because we were berated and abused by others. We thought the outside voice was our own, and we let it run roughshod over our lives. And then we judged ourselves for judging ourselves, trapped on a hamster wheel of self-flagellation. Oh, honey, that is no way to live. Without compassion for ourselves we will never stay on the road of radical self-love. Without compassion for others we can only replicate the world we have always known. Radical self-love is not about getting it right. "Getting it right" is a body-shame paradigm. Radical self-love is honoring how we are all products of a rigged system designed to keep us stuck in stigma and shame. The only way to beat that system is by giving ourselves something the system never will: compassion.

The four pillars of practice will support our personal radical self-love journeys, offering light along the road and helping us correct course when needed. If you use them in conjunction with the tools in the workbook, you will have much of what you need to build a daily thinking, doing, and being routine of radical self-love. I am totally jazzed for you . . . really! But our work together is not done. Now that we have done the work to transform our lives, it's time to take on the world!

4

A New Way
Ordered
by Love

A World for All Bodies Is a World for Our Bodies

Perhaps you have missed it thus far, but I have an agenda to which I am obnoxiously wedded. It's a simple agenda. I want to change the world by convincing you to love every facet of yourself, radically and unapologetically, even the parts you don't like. And through this work, illustrate for you how radical love alters our planet. Radical self-love is an internal process offering external transformation. How we show up to life reflects how we show up to ourselves. When we strip away the veneer of self-reliance and individualism and allow ourselves access to our most vulnerable truths, we can't help but be heartbeat present to the fact that our relationship with other bodies mirrors in tangible ways our relationship with our own body. Yes, we have been cutting and cruel to ourselves and have watched our internalized shame spill over into how we parent, how we manage employees, how we show up to friends and family. Yes, we believed that our bodies were too big, too dark, too pale, too scarred, too ugly, so we tucked, folded, hid ourselves away and wondered why our lives looked infinitesimally smaller than what we knew we were capable of. Yes, we have been less vibrant employees, less compassionate neighbors, less tolerant of the bodies of others, not because we are bad people but because we are guilty of each of those counts against ourselves.

Our lens to the outside world is an interior lens projecting our experience in our bodies onto our external landscape. A shame-clouded interior lens can only project shame and judgment. Employing a radical self-love ethos is like squirting glass cleaner on our daily lives: suddenly we can see ourselves as employees or em-

> **Radical Reflection**
>
> *The least compassionate politician and the most rigid authority figure are demonstrating to us how they are with themselves. We can practice compassion for them while demanding accountability from them.*

ployers, as parents and friends, as neighbors and community members, as leaders, thinkers, doers—as humans, distinctly connected to other humans. Applying radical self-love to each facet of these roles and responsibilities alters the very fabric of humanity, ultimately creating a more just, equitable, and compassionate world.

Speaking French and Implicit Bias

Bridging the gap between radical self-love and radical human love may feel like a Herculean task. "Sonya, it is hard enough to try this radical self-love stuff on myself! Now you want me to love the world?" What I am proposing is that radical human love is not an altruistic endeavor. We want a world that works for our bodies. There is one superhighway free of the debris of body shame and terror that gets us there, and that is radical human love. This means we must become the architects of a world that works for everybody and every body. Our responsibility to humanity is to unearth the ways in which we have been sabotaging the blueprints and thwarting the radical self-love efforts of others.

Right this minute, we are sauntering across someone's radical self-love path like a lumbering bovine. Removing ourselves as a barrier to other folks' radical self-love only becomes possible when we are willing to fear-facingly examine our beliefs. It is not enough to transform our relationship with our physical and emotional selves and leave the world around us unexamined or unaltered. Messages we received about the validity and invalidity of our own bodies did not occur in a vacuum. We were simultaneously receiving and spreading those messages. Dismantling oppression and our role in it demands that we explore where we have been complicit in the system of body terrorism while employing the same compassion we needed to explore our complicity in our internalized body shame. Regrettably, this is where too many of us choose to exit the radical self-love train. We desperately want our good intentions and niceness to be enough. Although each of us is inherently "enough" to be loved, valued, cared for, and treated with respect, our efforts to raze systems of oppression and injustice will require more than our niceness. "But I am a good person; I am nice to everyone" has never toppled one systemic inequity nor interrupted the daily acts of body terrorism leveled against humans throughout history. *You* are enough. Being good or nice is not.

Unapologetic Inquiry #22

Think of three times when your choice to be nice or polite made you complicit in body shame or body terrorism.

Why do we avoid looking at the ways in which we uphold systems of body shame and terror? For the exact same reasons, we avoid exploring uncomfortable thoughts about our own bodies and lives: we are in a constant struggle to distinguish our indoctrinated beliefs and behaviors from our true, radically self-loving beings. Remember that we are not the sum of our thoughts or even actions.

When we fail to make that distinction, we avoid exploring our ideas and continue to cause harm to ourselves and others. Seeing our thoughts and behaviors as part and not the whole of us allows us to transform our way of being with other bodies. In my "Ten Tools for Radical Self-Love" workshops, I describe our unconscious collusion with the system of body terrorism using the example of French.

If you were born into a francophone family, at around six to eight months of age you would utter your first mumbling word. Likely it would be *mère* (mother) or *père* (father) (if you're a really formal baby). Your language would be an extension of the world around you, which would likely consist of your French-speaking primary caregivers. Between eighteen months and two years of age, you would develop sentences. Again, those sentences would reflect the language you had been immersed in since birth. Unless your caregivers spoke or regularly exposed you to other languages, you undoubtedly would still be speaking French, even without ever having picked up a book or taken a single class. You would become a fluent French speaker. As you were exposed to more information, resources, and social systems, all in French, you would gain even greater proficiency. Your default language would be French. You'd think your thoughts in French. If you desired to learn a new language, you would have to study it, take classes, practice speaking it with others who had aptitude. It would take effort. On occasion, despite your new linguistic pursuits, you would return to speaking French. You might even subconsciously translate the new language back to French. Likely, no matter how proficient you became in another language, even if you stopped speaking French altogether, sometimes you would still think in French.

Body terrorism is our universal native tongue, our French. We learned the language in our formative years. We were the small child in the grocery store from Chapter 2, learning the language of ableism and being taught by our mothers to scurry off and whisper in shame and secrecy about the disabled body. We were five-year-old ballerinas in dance class being told by our teacher that we must wear nude tights with our leotards, only to discover that the default for "nude" in every store was pink or tan, never brown. It was in that class that we learned the default hierarchy of White bodies. We were children in the school cafeteria singing "Fatty, fatty, two by four, can't fit through the kitchen door." Or chanting "Keisha, Keisha Bald Spots" on the bus. Whether we chanted and sang along or not, we knew with certainty that we never wanted to be the people in those bodies being targeted. We learned the language of fatphobia and weight stigma, the language of difference-shaming. We were becoming fluent in body terrorism, either as perpetrators or as inactive bystanders, not because we were bad people but because we were in an immersion school of body shame. As adults, we have likely done much to disengage from the overtly callous messages we received about many bodies. But without an intentional free dive into the subconscious ways in which we still adhere to those beliefs, enact them in our lives, and project them onto the bodies of others, we will continue to speak body terrorism—ahem, French— whether we want to or not.

> **Radical Reflection**
>
> *When we practice awareness, we will notice that we "speak French" all day long. "What is that person wearing? She is too big to wear that!" "He needs to stop being such a wimp." The only way to stop speaking French is to notice when we are.*

Researchers have a term for the phenomenon I'm describing with my French analogy: implicit bias. The term refers to the "attitudes or stereotypes that affect our understanding, actions, and decisions in an unconscious manner."[1] Implicit bias can be favorable or unfavorable, but its key component is that it is involuntary: without an individual's conscious awareness or control. If you are prone to a heightened need for control, the concept of implicit bias might make your head explode. "What do you mean I am thinking things I don't think I'm thinking?" I know it can be trippy. Our brains are highly sophisticated organs encoding trillions of responses that control everything from scratching your head to jumping when someone startles you. Our embedded behaviors are so vast it would be impossible to notice them all. However, we do have the ability to raise some of these functions to conscious awareness.

Earlier we discussed the theory of in-group out-group bias. This theory can help us understand the origins of implicit bias and see its interruption as a pivotal tool in dismantling a world of body terrorism. Humans are predisposed to social categorization. We subconsciously evaluate who is part of our group and who is not. These assignments happen within seconds, directing our subsequent engagement and influencing our treatment of others. These biases most generously benefit the bodies we consider "normal" while fettering millions of folks on the path of radical self-love. None of us are solely culprits or solely victims. We all get a bit of what we give. Each person in a society is obstructing someone's road to radical self-love while simultaneously being obstructed on their own road. Sometimes we call this obstruction "privilege," which refers to the unearned benefits we receive in the world as a result of inhabiting some aspect of a default body. These areas of privilege lead to assumptions that the world is constructed only for specific bodies, while also failing to consider the experiences or needs of other bodies. It is thin privilege that installs the belief that if someone cannot fit in a chair at a restaurant, their body is the problem, not the manufacturer who made the chair or the restaurant owner who chose it. It is White privilege that would have us look around our workplace and boardrooms and think that creating tokens of a select few people of color who do not occupy positions of influence makes us a "diverse and inclusive" workplace. It is cisgender privilege that assigns the pronouns *she* and *he* to strangers based on ciscentric perceptions of their gender. Privilege and unexamined implicit bias upholds the hierarchy of bodies in our society, reaffirming our system of default bodies and codifying structures of body-based oppression. Implicit bias proves that just as we have internalized messages of body shame, so too have we been willful and unintentional agents of body terrorism. Through the exploration of how body shame has obstructed our own path, and by making a personal commitment to the creation of a just and compassionate world, we open up to the fear-facing examination of how our indoctrination has hindered the paths of others. Systems and structures of body terrorism are constructed, governed, and operated by humans—that is (cough, cough), by us. We built them, and only our intentional, concentrated efforts to deconstruct body terrorism in ourselves and in our world will tear them down.

Beating Body Terrorism from the Inside Out

Describing body terrorism as a systemic and structural issue underscores how our political, economic, and social systems uphold the marginalization of bodies based on race, gender, age, size, ability, sexual orientation, and a variety of other markers.

Unapologetic Inquiry #23

Destroying the system of body terrorism requires an investigation into our unconscious beliefs about other bodies. Remember, we are not our beliefs. We can examine them without judgment and shame. From a place of curiosity and compassion, explore the social, culture, and political messages you have received about the bodies listed below. How have those messages informed your relationship with those bodies?

- *Fat bodies*
- *Bodies of other races*
- *Lesbian or gay bodies*
- *Transgender bodies*
- *Disabled bodies*
- *Aging bodies*
- *Bodies with mental illness*

Bodies are not the only designators of oppression, but all oppression is enacted on the body. To discuss oppression as a manifestation of body terrorism is to move the conversation out of the abstract and return it to its site of impact, the body. Otherwise we risk forgetting that oppression in its many variations is a shared experience. Everybody with a body is affected. Understanding body terrorism as a function of systems and structures does not abdicate our responsibility for working toward its eradication. We do not get to say, "Oh well, racism/sexism/weight stigma/ageism/homophobia/transphobia is just so big. Boy, I sure hope 'they' figure it out." Systems do not maintain themselves; even our lack of intervention is an act of maintenance. Every structure in every society is upheld by the active and passive assistance of other human beings.

Let's take the example of body terrorism in the form of ableism. One structural manifestation of ableism is access. If you rented a space for an event and never considered whether that space had ramps, elevators, or disability restrooms, you would be individually upholding the system of ableism by not ensuring that a person with a disability could access your event. No, you didn't build the inaccessible building, but you did rent it, never considering its accessibility for all bodies, thus furthering the erasure of people with physical disabilities and their needs. The architects, investors, and builders who failed to include accessible accommodations for the building project participated in upholding the structural system of ableism by creating a barrier to access for people with disabilities in public life. Each of us is responsible for a sphere of influence. We are lawyers, salesclerks, teachers, loan officers, physicians, customer service representatives, counselors, judges, law enforcement agents— an inexhaustible list of humans whose jobs impact the lives of other humans every single day. As a human in a body sharing this planet with other humans in bodies, I have a responsibility to interrupt body terrorism, as do you.

This responsibility is distinct from some sort of savior complex in which radical self-love emboldens you to save the poor and downtrodden of Earth. Radical self-love is a manifestation of our interdependence. Lilla Watson, an Aboriginal Australian artist and activist, along with the activists of 1970s Queensland are credited with saying, "If you have come to help me, you are wasting your time. If you have come because your liberation is bound up with mine, then let us work together."[2] Our freedom from body terrorism is bound together. We each have a role in dismantling its systems and structures if we desire a free and spacious road to radical self-love. The first step is to interrupt the ways in which body terrorism resides in us.

Changing Hearts

Civil and labor rights activist Grace Lee Boggs died in 2015, leaving a legacy of work that exemplified her willingness to fear-facingly wrestle with how we create sustainable social change and justice. As a philosopher, she grappled with the delineation between rebellion and revolution. Her exploration of these nuances led her to focus her later writings on what she saw as an unyielding connection between our personal transformation and a transformed world. She wrote:

> Being a victim of oppression in the United States is not enough to make you revolutionary, just as dropping out of your mother's womb is not enough to make you human. People who are full of hate and anger against their oppressors or who only see Us versus Them can make a rebellion but not a revolution. . . . Therefore, any group that achieves power, no matter how oppressed, is not going to act differently from their oppressors as long as they have not confronted the values that they have internalized and consciously adopted different values.[3]

Boggs tells us that the only sustainable foundation for a changed world is internal transformation. We need look no further than our present political and social realities to see this premise in action. Social uprisings and upheaval are ineradicable foundations of human history. Laws, rules, and institutions are impermanent and fragile. They have been written, revised, and removed thousands of times over, and yet each new attempt at social change seems to be a mutation of a previous system of body terrorism. The PBS documentary *Slavery by Another Name* describes the post–Civil War practice of convict leasing: a system of leasing incarcerated people to local planters or industrialists in exchange for a minimal fee plus food and board.[4] Low initial cost to the people doing the leasing and increased revenue to the local prisons ballooned the practice, and soon wealthy entrepreneurs were buying and selling convicts between themselves. Laws like the Black Codes restricted Black life and freedom while disproportionately targeting Blacks for incarceration.[5] The body terrorism of slavery found its structural mutation in the form of convict leasing and Jim Crow laws. Today, mass incarceration serves the same function, according to legal scholar and author Michelle Alexander. She details the comparison in her groundbreaking book *The New Jim Crow:*

> In the era of colorblindness, it is no longer socially permissible to use race, explicitly, as a justification for discrimination, exclusion, and social contempt. So we don't. Rather than rely on race, we use our criminal justice system to label people of color "criminals" and then engage in all the practices we supposedly left behind. Today it is perfectly legal to discriminate against criminals in nearly all the ways that it was once legal to discriminate against African Americans. Once you're labeled a felon, the old forms of discrimination—employment discrimination, housing discrimination, denial of the right to vote, denial of educational opportunity, denial of food stamps and other public benefits, and exclusion from jury service—are suddenly legal. As a criminal, you have scarcely more rights, and arguably less respect,

than a black man living in Alabama at the height of Jim Crow. We have not ended racial caste in America; we have merely redesigned it.[6]

During the final years of the twenty-teens we saw a rise in body terrorism through xenophobic, nationalistic, and fascist-leaning governments politically targeting Muslims, Mexicans, Indigenous communities around the world, Black Americans, and other marginalized groups. From the anti-immigrant fueled departure of Britain from the European Union known as Brexit to Western countries denying refugees, to global protests challenging police brutality, we are experiencing the violent thrashing of a body-terrorism system near collapse. These actions recall a long history of state-sanctioned body terrorism. The Chinese Exclusion Act of 1882 placed a decade-long moratorium on the immigration of Chinese people into the United States, with the result of scapegoating them for the country's economic woes and limiting their rights for the next fifty years. Citing fears of Nazi spies, Franklin D. Roosevelt drastically limited the number of Jewish refugees allowed into the United States during World War II, taking less than a quarter of the twenty-six thousand he had authorized annually. This decision meant that in June 1939 the ocean liner SS *St. Louis*, which carried nearly one thousand Jewish passengers, was turned away from multiple ports and forced to return to Europe. More than a quarter of its passengers are believed to have been killed in the Holocaust.[7]

We do not have to travel far back through history to describe the shape-shifting nature of body terrorism. Homophobia and xenophobia led to an immigration ban in the United States against HIV-positive persons. The ban remained in place for more than two decades (until 2009), sanctioning social stigma and embedding it into foreign policy.[8] These legal and political decisions illuminate that shape-shifting power of centuries of body terrorism.

Why do we keep reinventing new forms of body terrorism? To answer that question, let's explore a conversation between former presidential candidate Hillary Clinton and a group of Black Lives Matter activists that took place in New Hampshire during the 2015 primaries. In a reportedly tense meeting, the soon-to-be Democratic nominee chided the young activists for what she saw as a naïve and unrealistic approach to addressing police violence against unarmed Black citizens. "Look, I don't believe you change hearts," Clinton said, arguing that the movement couldn't change deep-seated racism. "I believe you change laws; you change allocation of resources; you change the way systems operate. You're not going to change every heart. You're not."[9] Certainly, candidate Clinton felt she was offering sage advice at the time, highlighting the dangers of placing idealism above political pragmatism. Surprisingly, a year later Clinton released a campaign video in collaboration with the Human Rights Campaign that opens with her stating, "Equality is, of course, about changing laws, but it's also about changing hearts and minds."[10] Perhaps the final year on the campaign trail gave Hillary a peek into the true social and cultural consequences of our historical unwillingness to work to change hearts. Failing to change hearts makes body terrorism a centuries-old shell game of guessing what new law it is hiding beneath now.

In early 2020, dozens of Iranian and Iranian American U.S. citizens were detained at U.S. borders due to mounting tensions and a deadly airstrike on Iran by U.S. military forces. Washington governor Jay Inslee stated, "This is wrong and rife with constitutional and moral problems. No one should be treated differently due to where they come from, how they look, or what language they speak."[11] Body terrorism is not a historical aberration; it is the lived experience of far too many. As displaced Chinese immigrants, Jews turned away at port, Leelah Alcorn, and detained Iranian Americans would tell you if they could, the consequences of unchanged hearts are life and death. Body terrorism is made of both systems and structures, hearts and minds. It is the constant stratification of bodies, placing us into hierarchies where we are valued and denigrated—often at the same time, in the same body. Propagating a world of radical self-love is both a practice of individual transformation and a commitment to collective transformation. It is a practice of personal and global thinking, doing, and being. Radical self-love necessitates changed hearts, beginning with our own. Quite simply, we cannot build in the world that which we have not built in ourselves.

Unapologetic Agreements

Moving from a radical self-love that transforms you to a radical love that creates justice and equity in the world may feel like a tall order, but you are already on your way. As we cultivate new ways of being in our own bodies, we develop new ways of *being* on this planet with other bodies. A return to radical self-love requires our commitment to building shame-free, inclusive communities that uplift one another while honestly addressing body terrorism in all the ways it manifests as oppression based on age, race, gender, size, ability, sexual orientation, mental health status, and all other human attributes. Some will deride our efforts with charges of playing to "identity politics." We should remind those people that they, too, have identities that are informed by their bodies. Their lack of awareness about those identities generally means their body falls into a multiplicity of default identities that uphold the social hierarchy of bodies. The luxury of not having to think about one's body always comes at another body's expense. We should, with compassion, remind them that oppression oppresses us all, even those who are default. Not even they will always have a body at the top of the ladder. No one wins in a world of body terrorism.

At this very moment, someone is wringing their hands in worry. "But what if I make a mistake, Sonya? What if I say or do the wrong thing?" If it is you who is worrying, let me calm your precious nerves by assuring you that you *will* make a mistake . . . and then reminding you to revisit pillar 4. Creating a radical self-love world requires our willingness to have challenging conversations about privilege, power, history, culture, inequality, pain, and injustice. We will mess up and say something in French. That doesn't mean we quit. It also doesn't mean we become defensive and retreat to judgment and blame. It means we apologize and try again, holding fast to our intention to connect with other humans in different bodies from a place of compassion and shared humanity. As you move the conversation of radical self-love from an internal dialogue out into your family, community, and world, try on the Unapologetic Agreements that appear below. Commit to engaging in the type of radical self-love communication that grows our understanding of ourselves and one another—the type of communication that fosters global change.

1. **Be a body-shame-free friend.** Eliminate language that disparages bodies based on race, age, size, gender, ability, sexual orientation, religion, mental health status, or any other attribute. Compassionately challenge others you hear using body-shame language to describe themselves or others. This includes health or concern trolling (making unsolicited comments about a person's health based on their physical appearance).

2. **Engage and encourage curiosity-driven *dialogue*, not debate or arguing.** Practice the value of sharing and listening to the perspectives of others. The goal of dialogue need not be to change anyone's mind, but to *offer* and *receive* a perspective for consideration and curiosity.

3. **Embrace multiple perspectives.** Avoid having conversations from the assumption of right and wrong. Even if every cell in your body disagrees with someone's perspective, remember that making people "bad" and "wrong" will never build

connection and understanding. People who feel judged and attacked often only become further entrenched in their ideas.[12]

4. **Have compassion for and honor people's varied journeys.** Not everyone has read the books you've read or had the experiences you've had. There was a time when you had not had them either. Our journeys are unique and varied. Compassion births patience.

5. **Expect and accept discomfort.** Conversations about centuries-old oppressions are *hard*! If they were not, the world would be rid of body terrorism and oppression by now. Honor how we all have been indoctrinated into systems of oppression that we each must unlearn. Unlearning is challenging. Do not expect neat, tidy resolutions, or assume that we will instantly fix the world's ills in a single dialogue. We can, however, get closer to those goals if we are willing to be uncomfortable. Remember, fear is not necessarily danger.

6. **Acknowledge intent while addressing impact.** It is possible to be well-meaning and still cause harm. No matter our intention, we practice accountability when we are willing to acknowledge the impact of our words and actions on others. Likewise, people's words and behaviors may have an impact on us, but they are rarely actually about us. The way we respond to situations is most often a reflection of our own journey. Refraining from personalization makes accepting discomfort easier.

7. **Take breaks for self-care.** Talking with friends, family, and community about radical self-love, body terrorism, and body shame can be joyous and eye-opening. It can also be challenging and triggering. These conversations often involve issues that have caused great trauma in the world—and in our own lives. Some dialogues may bring up painful memories, old wounds, present hurts, and current resentments. We place a

premium on self-care as a tool of radical self-love! Do what you need to do to navigate your mental, emotional, and physical well-being. Step away from conversations when needed. Focus on yourself and come back when you are recentered. Radical self-love dialogue depends on your wellness.

8. **Interrupt attempts to derail.** Oftentimes, conversations about body terrorism and oppression bring up such discomfort that we immediately attempt to change the conversation to something that feels more comfortable. Before you know it, the conversation turns to pickle farmers in Europe when we started out talking about fat shaming. Work to keep the focus on the subject being addressed and avoid the desire to derail.

9. **Remember that personal attacks, name-calling, heavy sarcasm, and general unkindness are unhelpful.** The fastest way to devolve a dialogue is to turn to mean or hurtful language. Our anger need not be expressed as cruelty. We should work to speak from our "inside voice."

10. **Practice unapologetic inquiry.** Part of helping people sort through their ideas and beliefs is to ask questions about those ideas. That includes asking *ourselves* hard questions: "Why do I believe this? What am I afraid of? What am I gaining or losing by trying on a new perspective?" The answers that stick with us over time are the answers we come up with ourselves. Good questions get us to good answers.

11. **Have conversations based on what was actually said.** Often our translations of people's ideas are not accurate depictions of what they were sharing. Be sure to engage with people based on their actual words and not what you assume those words meant. If you are unsure, ask for clarity.

12. **Assume the best about one another.** It is exceptionally painful to be dismissed, called a liar, or accused of making up

your experiences. Start from the assumption that people's experiences are *real* and that they are the expert on their experience. We *may* have shared experiences, but this is not always true. Ask to learn more about other people's truths, rather than erasing them. Start from the assumption that we are all doing our best at any given moment with the tools we have.

13. **Celebrate difference.** Identifying difference is a way to embrace how we can all show up as our fullest, most authentic selves without shame. Acknowledge and embrace those things that are varied in us. Notice when difference is absent and investigate why. Ask who is not in the room. Our love of difference translates into creating a movement that welcomes everybody and every body.

14. **Make the goal of the conversation radical, unapologetic love.** The desire for a world free of body terrorism is a desire born out of love. Activist Che Guevara once said, "At the risk of seeming ridiculous, let me say that the true revolutionary is guided by a great feeling of love."[13]Allow your conversations to be guided by the primary principle of love.

"Sonya, will following these agreements keep me from arguing with my racist, fatphobic Aunt Martha during Thanksgiving dinner?" Listen, love, I cannot promise that you will never again storm out of the house and be forced to have your holiday meal of a bag of stale potato chips in your car. However, I can tell you that I have seen the Unapologetic Agreements transform hostility into human connection and acrimony into camaraderie. Like all radical self-love principles, they will take time and effort to master. But keep working at it. As they say in twelve-step programs, "You will be amazed before you are even halfway through."[14]

5

How to Fight with Love

I want you to know I have been holding your hand through this journey. I have been right there beside you as you've wrestled and pinned down your own fears and stood up to the bullying belief that somehow you were not enough. My ability to scale the mountainous task of writing an entire book about radical self-love has demanded I see you, not as some anonymous form, but truly see you, in your body, reading this book as the tremors of your own divine enoughness began to crack the ground of body shame around you. We need each other for this journey to be possible. Isolation is not solitude nor is it radical self-love. When we are connected to our own divine power, we become connected to all. That includes every other person who picked up this book and endeavored toward this work as well. The most transformative element of radical self-love is its ability to extend beyond our individual experience. You are not only reading this book to heal your own fraught relationship with your body. You are reading this book because you are called to pick up the needle and thread and add to the repair of our gorgeous but painfully tattered collective humanity. Together we can create a web of love, both energetic and material, psychological and physical. You have already begun weaving and it has imbued you with the planet-shifting force to fight a world of body terrorism through the transformative act of love.

Radical Self-Love Transforms Organizations and Communities

I propose that it is impossible to interact with radical self-love and remain unaltered. Once we are reconnected to our own radical self-love anchor, we start to register body-terrorism threats far more quickly. Our awareness of how body shame and body terrorism operate in our lives, families, communities, workplaces, and governments becomes acute and uncomfortable, like lying on a bed of body-shame cacti. It is this discomfort on a community and organizational level that motivates structural change. In publishing this book, I had the opportunity to see firsthand how a radical self-love framework pushes an organization out of their corporate comfort zone and into the realm of the radical. This sort of organizational shift is essential if we want to bring about long-term systemic and structural change.

Berrett-Koehler Publishers is the awesome midsized independent publishing house who brought you this book. Based in Oakland, California, their mission is "connecting people and ideas to create a world that works for all." We were clearly cosmically suited for one another, and I was an enthusiastic YES when they approached me about writing a book on the work of radical self-love. Berrett-Koehler's commitment to being equitable, fair, and focused on positive change was beautiful. But beautiful is not necessarily radical. Somehow encountering the radical self-love message always seems to plant seeds whose fruits come to bear, often unexpectedly.

The humans working to bring the TBINAA book to life were as diverse as my former poetry slam team all those years ago. Jeevan, a tall, Brown, South Asian man with whom it appeared I had as much in common as a watermelon has with a wombat, was assigned as my editor. He was patient as the winds of imposter syndrome whipped me into a ball of worry and procrastination. Although kind, he was not yet a radical self-love convert. "The truth is . . ." Jeevan confessed, "I wasn't sure I even agreed with her—it was too easy to dismiss her (initially) as yet another 'fat-positive' person who was trying to force others to support something that was flawed, unhealthy, and making excuses for just poor life choices. I did agree to work on the book, though, because someone whom I respect deeply told me once that every editor should work on books he or she disagrees with, because to do otherwise was unacceptable to our role as disseminators of a truly wide spectrum of ideas."

Many of us start off like Jeevan, skimming the surface of radical self-love based on our preconceived notions and historical biases. We treat new ideas like we treat bodies, dismissing what we can't understand, what we view as too different. Luckily for me, Jeevan's job description demanded that he get below the surface of this radical self-love concept. What he discovered lying at the bottom of his own ocean floor was a history of disordered eating, stories of body shame he harbored against himself, and judgment he aimed at others. Months after the book went to print, Jeevan shared the following with me:

> Working on this book impacted me more deeply than almost 95 percent of all the books I have ever worked on (keeping in mind that I have indirectly and directly been involved to some level in over 400 books by now). This book is not about something as simple as body positivity or acceptance. It is about the ways in which we see others and ourselves and judge one another on far deeper levels than we may know because at the heart of it all, even the deepest-held beliefs begin with the most superficial and perfunctory glances and barely conscious judgments. The deepest

convictions we hold and the ways in which we interact and treat one another are often put in place there by the seemingly most superficial of assessments—those of others' bodies and our own.

Jeevan had awakened to how radical self-love might heal us from these barely conscious judgments. He began to see how its properties might act as a salve on the many other oppressive afflictions plaguing our world. What Jeevan didn't know was that he was about to slather a heap of radical self-love on his whole workplace.

Everyone's radical self-love boundaries were pushed wide open when it came time to pick a cover for this book. I'd walked into the planning meeting toting a laptop folder full of meek and mild Pinterest images and color themes meant to evoke feelings of freedom, love, and connection. I was not thinking radically. But when I cursorily flashed the image of my naked body sprawled against a background of purple hydrangeas, the room audibly gasped. The picture was one in a series of photos titled "American Beauty" that featured trans and cis women of different ethnicities, body sizes, and aesthetics re-creating the iconic scene from the 1999 film of the same name. Photographer Carey Fruth's viral photos snatched beauty back from the singular American thin, blonde, young, White, cisgendered ideal and placed it on a fat, dark-skinned, bald Black woman.

"That is the cover, Sonya," Jeevan pronounced to the conference room of staff.

"Umm, Jeevan, I really am not prepared to be naked in Barnes and Noble," I shot back.

"Sonya, this photo is what this book is saying. That it is okay to be you, in your body, even if that body is naked."

"But it's not about me. I don't want people to see a fat Black woman on the cover and decide not to buy the book," I retorted. There, as naked as my book cover, were the boundaries of my own radical self-love: the fear that my body would mean rejection. Even if I didn't see my body as wrong, what if the world did? My editor had resurrected my original hypothesis. Either my unapologetic image would imbue others with the power and permission to be unapologetic in their bodies or I would be judged, rejected, shrunk down, and contained. The only way to know was to broaden the potential of radical self-love and see if others could withstand the pressure.

Once my scantily clad cover was released for feedback, Berrett-Koehler's boundaries were tested as well. Amid the emphatic affirmations for the cover were also "concerns" that the images might be seen as pornographic or erotic. Marketers said they would have to deliver the book in black plastic as "adult content" with reps in Brazil, proposing the image was too racy. Yup, BRAZIL! When Berrett-Koehler higher-ups expressed concern that the image might be objectifying and sexualized, Jeevan responded like a budding radical self-love scholar pointing out the double standard in the perception of my dark, large body compared to other book covers showcasing naked thin White women. He even identified how it is not men's roles to tell women, and in this case women of color, whether or not they are being objectified and encouraged men in the company to listen to the perspectives of women of color.

Berrett-Koehler put the Three Peaces into practice in order to bring this book to the world. The team had to make peace with my different body on the cover and the necessity for a different creative process to bring this book to market, honoring that the message of radical self-love demanded more than standard operating procedure. Secondly, they had to make peace with not understanding and allowing others to not understand too. Not every team member or partner would get why I needed to be naked on the cover of the book and nor did they need to in order to bring this project to fruition. The organization did need to trust the judgment of the team members who did understand. By choosing to raise to prominence and listen to the voices of women, and specifically women of color, on this project, Berrett-Koehler decentered the default bodies in their organization and relinquished the need to control the process, creating space to trust that there were simply parts of the journey they would not understand—and that it was not something to fear.

Lastly, Jeevan's journey of making peace with his own body and reflecting on how he'd spent so many years apologizing helped him shepherd his organization through the Three Peaces. His own radical self-love journey became the foundation for his organizational advocacy. Others followed suit and encouraged even deeper reflection and through the collective process brought about company-wide shift in perspective. I'd like to think Berrett-Koehler is getting a bit more radical by the day.

Freedom Frameworks for an Unapologetic Future

It bears repeating again, this book does not propose that razing body shame and body terrorism in ourselves or out in the world is easy. If it were, I'd be on to my horticulture career by now. Unfortunately, there is an ultimate warrior obstacle course of barriers we must circumnavigate to effectively transform a world run by the Body-Shame Profit Complex into a world that supports our diverse and divine bodies. Luckily for us, a plethora of brilliant and beautiful humans have lent their light as guidance on the path. They are the candle keepers, friends and peers whose wisdom offers consistent direction on the pathway toward a just, equitable, and compassionate planet for each of us.

Pleasure activist, doula, and social-justice facilitator adrienne maree brown's work puts us in powerful conversation with two essential elements in creating a radical self-love world: the power of emergent strategy and the radical power of pleasure. In her book *Emergent Strategy: Shaping Change, Changing Worlds*, adrienne maree brown identifies how the simple interactions of the natural world offer us insight into myriad possibilities for collective social change. She puts forth a series of principles that undergird the framework of emergent strategy. Her ninth principle holds the full intention of this radical self-love work in its simple offering: "What you pay attention to grows."[1] If our collective focus becomes love and the notion that every human being in every imaginable form deserves a world where they can love and be loved in the bodies they have today . . . and if the definition of love is one that includes resource, care, compassion, justice, and safety for all bodies, just imagine what we might grow together!

Leah Lakshmi Piepzna-Samarasinha's work as a queer, disabled femme of color continues to bring to the center the stories, lives, and needs of queer, sick and disabled, BIPOC bodies. In her book *Care Work*, Leah illustrates how sick and disabled folks practice radical love by celebrating the networks of care their communities have cultivated throughout history for survival. She makes visible how the imperfect but innovative organizing of sick, mad, neurodivergent, crip, d/Deaf, and disabled folks of color continuously challenge systems of body terrorism beyond ableist binary notions of sad or "inspiring." Leah reminds us that the disability community has been one of our most enduring examples of what it means to leave no body behind and that care work and radical self-love are inextricably bound. She offers:

> Love is bigger, huger, more complex and more ultimate than petty fucked up desirability politics. We all deserve love. Love as an action verb. Love in full inclusion, in centrality, in not being forgotten. Being loved for our disabilities, our weirdness, not despite them. . . . Love gets laughed at. What a weak, non-political, femme thing. Bullshit, I say. Making space accessible as a form of love is a disabled femme of color weapon.[2]

Leah and adrienne are two of hundreds of humans I watch in real time embodying a radical self-love praxis through new and existing frameworks. Radical self-love, disability justice, emergent strategy, and pleasure activism are unique dialects for a co-manifested world brimming with the abundant opportunities, access, and resources any of us may need to evince our divine purpose, whatever that may be. Leah's essay on making space accessible as an act of love was written the same year I wrote the poem "The Body Is Not an Apology." Perhaps we were all being simultaneously directed to add to the elixir of radical healing needed to actualize a new unapologetic future for us all. You are also being called to add to the brew.

Fighting Oppression, Isms, and Phobias

Together we have examined how the systems of body shame and body terrorism live in us and how we might demolish them from the inside. Radical self-love starts with us but was never meant to end there. The internal practice is for the purpose of envisaging a new world order guided by love. How we get there requires we fight the systems of body shame and hierarchy individually and interdependently, both committing to personal accountability and lending strength to the collective battle against body terrorism. In the remaining pages are strategies, candle keepers, and radical self-love warriors to follow and organizations to support with your money and time. To fight such deeply ingrained systems we must be willing to do both internal and external work, working on our indoctrinations and working with others to further the initiatives and efforts that have long been pushing for justice, equity, and systemic change. As Leah reminds us, we will need the most powerful weapon in human history . . . love.

Fighting Fatphobia

Fatphobia remains one of the most challenging forms of body terrorism to beat back. The multibillion-dollar weight loss and diet industry has figured out how to squeeze into every crevice of our lives more effectively than a pair of Spanx, using fear, shame, and a co-opted "body positivity" to sell us more deceptively marketed fad diets through fatphobic narratives of "getting healthy" and "lifestyle" changes. From corporate, employment, and immigration discrimination against fat people to the erasure and gaslighting of fat people daily in doctor's offices, our bias against fat is consistently wreaking personal, professional, and structural terror on fat people's lives. Research repeatedly shows that weight stigma and bias lead to ongoing substandard care by medical professionals. Lifesaving diagnoses go undetected and vital care is often refused to those with fat bodies.[3] Couple this reality with medical bias against women, trans and gender-nonconforming folks, and people of color and imagine what the medical experience of a fat trans woman of color might be like (cue the intersectional analysis). Fat is not the problem; fatphobia is what is deadly.

How can we fight fatphobic body terrorism? As with all radical self-love change, we must start with us. The recipe is simple (though not easy): explore and challenge our assumptions (thinking), shift our actions (doing), and develop an emanating self-love practice (being). Using our thinking, doing, being approach, we can challenge fatphobia in ourselves and call in others to do the same.

Thinking
Strategy 1: Embrace Shame-Free Inquiry
There is no better place to start than to get curious about what we currently believe and how we may be operating as unwitting agents of body terrorism. Shame is a big burdensome iron bar that will keep you from your curious quest before you even begin. Be inquisitive and loving rather than harsh with yourself and your answers. Remember, you are not bad or wrong—you're human.

Below are questions to help you explore your thoughts and beliefs about fat bodies:

- Do I believe it's okay to be bigger, just not too big? How do I define "too big"?
- Do I make assumptions about people's health based on their weight?
- Do I believe "healthier" bodies are better bodies?
- Do I use the word *fat* pejoratively to describe myself or others (including internal dialogue)?
- Do I believe being fat is fine for others, just not for me?
- Do I believe fat people could lose weight if they just tried hard enough?
- Am I afraid of becoming fat?
- Do I dislike my own fat?

If you answered yes to any of these questions, you have some internalized fatphobia to work on. Here's the good news... of course you do! As I mentioned in Chapter 4, it would be a feat of supernatural proportions for you to grow up in a fatphobic society and not have internalized fatphobic ideas. But now that you have raised those fatphobic thoughts and beliefs to consciousness you are ready to step into new action.

Doing

Strategy 2: Make Fat Familiar

We live in a fatphobic culture that assigns default status to thin bodies while labeling all others abnormal, unhealthy outliers. Shake up the paradigm by becoming familiar with the lives and experiences of fat people. Look around your life. Is it filled with smaller bodied people? Are your bookshelves lacking in fat protagonists by fat authors? Who are the fat heroes and heroines on your television? Are they empowered or do they spend their scenes chasing thinness? How about your social media feed? Following any fat folks? If not, today is the day to fatten your timeline. Becoming familiar with the lives of fat people helps to normalize fat bodies and makes us all more aware of what they traverse to survive in a fatphobic world. You are better positioned to challenge fat bias and weight stigma when you have proximity to the lives of fat people.

Listen, fight fatphobic foolishness, but your newsfeed and bookshelf shouldn't be a Wikipedia of sad, fat lives of discrimination and trauma. Why? Because fat people are thriving in their bodies. Making fat familiar means bearing witness to fat bodies in joy, pleasure, desire, nature, rest, love, movement, and nourishment. Friend, activist, and aptly titled King of the South Jazmine Walker leads a national body movement workshop called "Praise and Twerkship" where she helps Black people reclaim the sensual magic of movement in their bodies. Her Instagram (@jazonyamine) is a visual feast of Jazmine's morning ritual of twerking and dancing alone in her home. Transformation as magic is watching a fat Black woman from the South cast the spell of her own bounce and rhythm. Jazmine is teaching us to not only accept the fat Black body but to worship it. Taking new action means celebrating the presence of fat bodies more loudly than we applaud the infinite endeavors to shrink our bodies.

Being

Strategy 3: Practice in Public

The practice of new and repeated action is how we step into a radical self-love way of being. To do this, we must practice regularly disrupting fatphobia and weight stigma out loud in our daily lives. If you have spent years on the diet hamster wheel, it is a great day to ditch diet culture and practice a loving, gentle relationship with your body. Intuitive Eating[4] and Health at Every Size (HAES)[5] are two alternative models moving us away from diet culture and toward providing your body the nourishment and care that is best for you. Both models have principles that turn our attention to our original control center, our bodies, where we can receive the internal cues that lead us to personally defined well-being informed by our unique bodies. Rethink your orientation to food and health. Share your journey with your friends and family to practice in public.

Fatphobia remains one of the most underdiscussed and unacknowledged forms of body terrorism. The allure of thin privilege is frighteningly persuasive; from easy shopping to better job and romantic opportunities, society promotes and rewards thinness and punishes fat. The pernicious lie of fatness as an individual failure of self-control, lack of discipline, evidence of gluttony and laziness all wrapped in a scientifically unsound narrative of health often leads even the most vocal intersectional social justice activists to promote weight loss and advance fatphobic body terrorism. Stomping out fatphobia will mean challenging our friends', families', and coworkers' indoctrination by questioning stereotypes, sharing what we are learning about fatphobia, and asking others to learn with us.

You can start by exploring the racist, classist roots of our societal beliefs about fat bodies by reading *Fearing the Black Body: The Racial Origins of Fat Phobia*[6] by scholar Sabrina Strings. Consider alternatives to that family or companywide weight loss challenge by sharing information about intuitive eating and Health at Every Size. Speak up when you see your friends lauding weight loss as achievement and let them know how "before and after" pictures present "before" bodies as wrong and "after" bodies as better. Financially support organizations like the Association for Size Diversity and Health (ASDAH)[7] and NOLOSE[8] that center the dignity and freedom of fat people. Follow and learn from fat people who are living unapologetically fat lives and promote their work. We all live for Lizzo, and even she would want you to widen your repertoire. Remind everyone that body positivity began as a movement for fat liberation led by and for fat people and must continue to center them. Love fat people out loud and in public and demand others do the same. By joining this fight, you are helping to tear down the bricks of body terrorism one fatphobic idea at a time.

Fighting Ableism

Much like fatphobia and intersectional in its manifestations is our abhorrent social, political, and economic treatment of those living with disabilities, chronic illness, neurodivergence, and other mental health conditions. Under a capitalist system, disabled bodies and differently working brains are difficult to exploit for profit and thus have been framed as bad bodies that should be hidden, pitied, or, as with the eugenics movement, murdered. When they are not met with violence, we use disabled bodies as "inspiration porn," presenting their bodies as the reason able-bodied people should be more grateful. To defeat an ableist world, we must first look at how we participate in perpetuating one.

Thinking

Strategy 1: Embrace Shame-Free Inquiry

It is easy to point out all of the things wrong with the world. It is a much more uncomfortable and courageous task to look at how we too have been complicit in the maintenance of systems of body terrorism. In a society incredibly adept at harsh and often cruel critique, it is deeply moving to witness one tending to their own culpability with a sense of humility, compassion, and grace. It restores faith in the possibility that perhaps they will extend the same grace and compassion to me. It is from this extension that we often feel safe enough to transform. Get acquainted with how ableism lives in you and your everyday life. Consider the following questions for exploration:

- Do I or have I ever thought about, asked about, or endeavored to learn about the lives of disabled people?

- Do I think about whether my surroundings either at home or work are accessible to those with physical or intellectual disabilities or processing differences?
- Do I have disabled, chronically ill, or neurodivergent people in my personal or professional life?
- Do I assume disabled people hate their bodies? Do I pity them?
- Do I use ableist language like lame, blind, dumb, crazy, insane, nuts, or crippled?
- Have I or do I refer to disabled people as inspiring?
- Would I be ashamed if I had a mental health diagnosis?

Answering these questions helps us assess how commonplace ableism is in our daily lives. Black disability activist Imani Barbarin created the hashtag #abledsareweird to give voice to the barrage of ableist experiences disabled folks are subjected to regularly. Visit the hashtag on Twitter and inventory your own behaviors. If you are able-bodied, it is inevitable that ableist messages have influenced how you perceive disability and illness. Getting into some anti-ableist action is the surest route to divesting from ableism and helping others do the same.

Doing
Strategy 2: Dig into Disability Justice
We can have a world free of ableism, but getting there requires the leadership, guidance, and visionary brilliance of disabled, mad, and chronically ill people. Like most movements for justice, those most impacted have the answers. If we directed our attention and re-sources to supporting them, we'd be far closer to freedom. The disability justice movement was conceived by a group of "black, brown, queer and trans" people which included leaders like Patty Berne, Leroy F. Moore Jr., Mia Mingus, the late Stacey Milbern, and others

involved in the radical disability arts organization SINS Invalid.[9] Disenchanted by how the modern disability rights movement too often centered the experiences and needs of White disabled people, this coalition of the marginalized developed a framework to highlight how ableism was intricately woven into racism, queer and trans phobia, and sexism and understood that abolishing one would necessitate abolishing all forms of oppression. Disability Justice offers ten principles to build upon a more inclusive, accessible, and just world for all our bodies. Some of these include:

- Leadership of the Most Impacted: "We are led by those who most know these systems" (Aurora Morales).
- Recognizing Wholeness: People have inherent worth outside of commodity relations and capitalist notions of productivity. Each person is full of history and life experience.
- Interdependence: We meet each other's needs as we build toward liberation, knowing that state solutions inevitably extend to further control over lives.
- Collective Liberation: No body or mind can be left behind. Only mobbing together can we accomplish the revolution we require.[10]

Learn and spread the Disability Justice framework. Utilize these principles in your daily life and invite others to do the same. Dismantling ableism means digging into this intersectional, cross-solidarity movement and doing your part to leave no body behind.

Being

Strategy 3: Practice in Public

Taking action against ableism requires actively engaging the perspectives of disabled people of all identities in your life. Read, listen, and watch media that centers disabled lives not as feel-good stories for able-bodied folks' consumption but as works that present disabled people in the full complexity of their lives, made for and by them. Challenge casual ableism by asking about accessibility in the places you frequent. Interrupt the ableist language you use and enroll others in doing the same. Invite those you love to be part of raising awareness and action to be in greater solidarity with disabled communities. Similar to fatphobia, activist spaces often erase the needs of the disability community, fighting for the rights of LGBTQIAA+ and/or people of color, while forgetting that many of those people are or will be disabled. Activism absent of the voices and vision of disabled people cannot be radical. Disabled people should be part of the leadership and planning of our work, and if they are not we must ask why.

Queer, fat, disabled TBINAA staff writer Nomy Lamm suggested we add access needs to our digital staff meeting check-ins alongside our names and pronouns. Team members were given time to consider what they needed or what the team should know to aid in their fullest participation in the meeting. A teammate had chronic pain and said they would need to step away to stretch during the call. Another shared how their depressive episode was impacting their information processing and might need folks to repeat themselves. Others had sensory processing challenges and asked that we type in chat so they could be on mute and still participate in the meeting. Some people had no access needs in April but needed support on the call in May. Through this practice we normalized access needs by making space to consider them and ask for support. At some point all humans will have access needs. Practice identifying them and asking for them to be met. Are you a visual learner who'd benefit from someone writing down what they are saying on flipchart paper? Maybe you feel claustrophobic and need a door to be opened during the meeting? Perhaps you have chemical sensitivities and need people to refrain from using perfumes and chemical fragrances? Much like wheelchair spaces, ramps, and ASL interpreters, these too are access needs. When we normalize access needs, we destigmatize difference, carving out space for invisible disabilities and illnesses in our communities. This is how we interrupt the abled body as the default body. Practicing in public means making disability part of how you think, live, and love in the world and asking friends, family, community, and your workplace to join you in doing the same.

Fighting Queerphobia and Transphobia

Our indoctrination into cis- and hetero-centrism begins before we are even born. From gender reveal parties to color-coded baby showers, society compels our allegiance to strict gender and sexual roles before our first breath. Those who fail to comply with our default assumptions of gender as male or female and sexuality as attraction to the opposite gender are maligned, erased, and, throughout history, killed with little recourse. We have constructed our social, political, and economic systems to value cisgender people—those who identify with the gender they were assigned at birth—and privilege them in ways that go unnoticed. The reality for a disproportionate number of queer, trans, and gender-nonconforming people globally is that of unrelenting body terrorism, with even higher rates for queer and trans Black, Indigenous, and people of color (QTBIPOC).

Thinking

Strategy 1: Embrace Shame-Free Inquiry

From a place of curiosity and compassion, explore how you have made cisgender and heterosexual identity the default in your life. Consider the following questions:

- Do I make assumptions about people's gender based on what they are wearing or look like?
- Do I assume people's gender without asking them, using he or she pronouns based on only my assessment?

- Do I have transgender people in my personal or professional life?
- When I meet married people, do I assume their partner is of the opposite gender?
- Do I follow, read, or watch content created by LGBTQIAA+ people?
- Do I use gendered terms like "ladies and gentlemen" when speaking?
- Do I equate being a woman or a man to genital or reproductive body parts?

Lesbian, gay, bisexual, transgender, queer, questioning, intersex, asexual, agender, pansexual, polyamorous, kink, two-spirit . . . if you read this list and feel overwhelmed, imagine what it might be like to spend most of your life being invisible in film, television, radio, schools, jobs, and so on. When you are represented, it is to provide stereotypical comic relief, sensationalism (see Jerry Springer), or mockery. In fact, there are infinite arrangements for how we experience or don't experience attraction, desire, and understand our gender. Still we scoff at the rolling out of so many letters, never questioning who we have been erasing and shrinking into a dry binary default. A world free of queerphobic and transphobic body terrorism obligates us to look at our own privilege and investment in only considering the default bodies of cis and straight people.

Doing
Strategy 2: Queer Your Life
Black Canadian poet Brandon Wint's viral quote offers a foundation upon which to begin queering our perspectives with a new radical definition of queer. "Not queer like gay. Queer like, escaping definition. Queer like some sort of fluidity and limitlessness at once. Queer like a freedom too strange to be conquered. Queer like the

fearlessness to imagine what love can look like and pursue it."[11] Brandon's quote helps us reconceptualize queerness, expanding it beyond the boundaries of sex and desire, moving it into the realm of the uncontainable. If radical self-love is an act of becoming difference celebrating then pursuing a "freedom too strange to be conquered" is right up the radical self-love alley. In order to compost[12] homophobia and transphobia into the rich soil of radical self-love, we must begin to challenge the subtle and not-so-subtle ways it governs our world.

Get intimate with the lives and struggles of queer and trans people. It's tempting to assume that the visibility of Caitlin Jenner and the achievement of same-sex marriage of cisgender people means we have solved homo- and transphobia. But visibility and the legal right to marry are both privileges afforded those with the most access and other intersecting default identities, such as Whiteness or wealth. Media would make it appear that the transgender community sprouted overnight. What the Western world understands as transgender identity has been around throughout history,[13] and the term *transgender* is a Western conceptualization we have created to make sense of expanded gender identity beyond the constraints of a binary. Other cultures have long had members of their societies who have lived outside the confines of simply male or female, and our efforts to interrupt body terrorism demands we queer our understanding of gender.

Also paramount to queering our lives is learning about the lives of the contemporary trailblazers who forged a path for queer and trans rights, including the names and histories of folks like Marsha P. Johnson and Sylvia Rivera, two trans women of color who were instrumental in the Stonewall uprisings—the resistance protests that sparked the gay rights movement[14] on Turtle Island (U.S.). Raise attention and awareness to the alarmingly high rate of murders of Black and Latinx trans women and explore the connection between their mortality and society's discriminatory and violent treatment of trans people. Support, promote, and resource action and acknowledgment days like Transgender Day of Remembrance.[15] But do not stop there. Ask tough questions like, "Would we need a Transgender Day of Remembrance if we practiced vocally celebrating and creating access and resource for trans and gender-nonconforming people in the present?" Queering our lives means challenging heterosexuality and cisgender identity as superior or normal ways of being. As we continue to center the lives of queer and trans people, inevitably we do exactly what Brandon proposed: we become cocreators of a "freedom too strange to be conquered."

Being

Strategy 3: Practice in Public

Social change is not automatically tied to personal change. Nice as it would be, it is not a given that the systems of body terrorism will instantly dematerialize just because we become less harmful to ourselves and those around us. Nope. We must use our newfound power to communally push those systems down with organized, collective action. Some of our efforts will be small and interpersonal, like interrupting queer and transphobic stereotypes we hear from friends, family, or coworkers. And other efforts will need to target structural and systemic issues.

In a system that devalues the lives of queer and trans people and to an even greater extent queer and trans Black, Indigenous, and people of color, organizations created and led by the QTBIPOC community are often the most underfunded and under-resourced. Using our dollars to help support communities carving out lives of dignity and respect in the face of constant body terrorism is a necessary radical self-love practice *and* an act of best-interest buying. Following their leadership and guidance and encouraging others to follow suit helps build those organizations' capacity and further their impact. Show up and volunteer at an LGBTQIAA+ youth center, and support queer- and trans-led media, music, and content. Support the basic needs of someone in the queer and trans community who is struggling, perhaps by contributing to their crowdsourcing campaigns. These are all personal actions that strengthen the collective, but you can and should also act in advocacy in places where you have privilege. You can disrupt the binary default at work by sharing your gender pronouns and asking your coworkers to share theirs, even if—especially if—you assume everyone is cisgender. Ask your employer about their hiring practices and whether or not they have considered if the workplace is queer and trans inclusive. If it is not, push for equity and inclusion initiatives at your organization. Be sure to do this before you begin inviting queer and trans people into hostile work environments. Challenge queer and transphobic legislation by writing your government representatives and keeping abreast of local and national bills that might affect the lives of the queer and trans people most often left behind. Practice in public asks us to put our individual and collective efforts toward creating a just and generous world for trans and queer people. Until all of us are free, none of us is free.

Fighting Racial Inequity

In Chapter 2, we discussed how the notion of default bodies shapes how we perceive our own bodies and impacts the experiences of all human bodies. In Chapter 4, we explored how body terrorism builds structures and systems that privilege default bodies and marginalize bodies of difference. Some of the most pervasive, violent, and longstanding forms of body terrorism are racism, White supremacist delusion, and racial inequity. There are reams of books, workshops, podcasts, speaker talks, and films to help you understand and unpack how racism—and specifically White supremacist delusion—impacts the world and the lives of people of color. I won't reinvent the wheel when so much genius currently exists in this area. There are, however, a few vital points I believe will help us all as we strategically work to rid the world of racist White supremacist body terrorism.

Thinking

Strategy 1: Equity above Equality

Abolishing racism means that we must be fear-facing and examine our complicity and indoctrination. We've been complicit—not out of malice but because we have been groomed and raised in a system of racial injustice that has relied on our obliviousness and/or apathy to maintain its uninterrupted operation. You may notice that I did not use the term *racial inequality* to describe the outcomes of racism in our society but instead chose *racial inequity*. Equity and equality achieve significantly different ends for those who experience and live with the impacts of racism. Equality means providing the same opportunities or levels of support to everyone—a well-intentioned practice on the surface. But if we peel back a layer we can see how the guise of equality can spread inequity like a brush fire. Consider you were hosting an eight-month-old baby, an eighty-five-year-old woman, and a twenty-two-year-old man for dinner tomorrow night (I know it's weird to host a baby for dinner, but bear with me). Would you feed them all a roast lamb entrée? How about a single tall glass of fresh breast milk? My hunch is you would know that each of these humans needs considerably different options for their very different bodies. Feeding them equally in amount or type of food would not be an act of truly caring for any of them. Equity proposes that we give people what they need to best meet their unique circumstances. Equity acknowledges we have varying needs and seeks to provide resource and opportunity based on what will help us achieve the best outcomes based on our specific circumstances.[16] Racial equity honors how histories of racism, White supremacist ideologies, slavery, and colonization have altered the playing field, leaving many racial groups to navigate issues that demand a different set of solutions. Working toward racial equity may mean releasing our outdated notions of fair and working toward creating systems and structures that are just.

Doing

Strategy 2: Wake Up to Racism and White Supremacist Delusion

In most of the Western world and nations impacted by colonization, bodies that are coded as "White" are given default status and the privileges and systemic power of said status. People of color, whether they be Black, Latinx, Indigenous, Asian, Middle Eastern, Pacific Islander and all others, have been systemically discriminated against globally, resulting in disparate outcomes in wealth, health, education, and most other social markers of capitalism.

In Ijeoma Oluo's book *So You Want to Talk about Race*, she explains why it is useful to define racism as the experience of race-based prejudice plus the power of a system that codifies those prejudices under misleading, neutralized terms (recall our discussion of color blindness).[17] If you are reading this book, I'm going to venture that you are not a neo-Nazi. Which is great, but you don't need to be a neo-Nazi to help the system of White supremacist racism carry on. You simply have to do nothing, and the powerful mechanisms of racial body terrorism will continue to operate with relative ease and efficiency.

If you are White or present as White, like it or not you will receive benefits from society because of your racial identity. The most effective way to ensure no one else ever gets the benefits you get is to never question why you get those benefits. In the fourteen-part podcast series *Seeing White*, hosts John Biewen and Chenjerai Kumanyika carry listeners through the inception, codification, and proliferation of White identity as default, embarking on an ocean-deep exploration into how Whiteness came into being, from the invention of the mythical race science to its accumulation of power.[18]

Unfortunately, White supremacist delusion has not only shaped how White people operate around race. It has shaped how people of color see, understand, and experience themselves and other communities of color. Global anti-Blackness, the Asian model-minority myth, colorism, xenophobia, and Islamophobia are all fueled by the toxic outgrowths of the internalized White supremacist narratives BIPOC hold about each other. By divesting in White supremacist narratives of fearing otherness, we can reinvest our time in learning about the struggles, lives, and liberation stories of other people of color. It is in our solidarity that we can topple the system of White supremacist delusion.

Being
Strategy 3: Muscle Up and Join In
If you live in a privileged body, it's likely you have not been forced to think about the blinders of privilege. Society allows your default body to exist without considering the ways in which that default status impacts others or, for that matter, impacts you. White people are rarely asked to think about their Whiteness. Consequently, when people of color discuss the weight of racial injustice, it is often White people who buckle in guilt, shame, denial, minimization, and any number of other tactics to avoid accountability. This avoidance is not only gaslighting and exhausting for people of color, it simultaneously robs White people of the opportunity to explore and interrupt the ways they assist in propping up the system of White supremacy. This atrophied racial muscle has been called *white fragility*,[19] but what if we centered how People of Color experience the behavior, rather than how white people experience it? In that context, it might be more aptly titled *white violence*. Dismantling the edifices of White supremacist delusion will require that White people build intellectual and

emotional honesty in matters of race. It's time to develop a radical racial workout.

Despite their best efforts, White people will never be the most proficient at identifying the machinations of White supremacist delusion any more than subjects in a picture would be adept at pointing out the details of the frame. As is frequently noted, it is not the job of people of color to explain racism to White people. Yet people of color have generously provided exhaustive, nuanced, and detailed resources in the form of scholarship, literature, film, television, music, visual art, providing an ark of resources to help White people abandon the ideology and artifices of White supremacy. One such act of gift is author Layla Saad's Instagram challenge turned workbook turned *New York Times* best-selling title, *Me and White Supremacy*. Saad offers readers a twenty-eight-day workbook to explore how White supremacy intersects and influences White people's lives, asking readers to confront anti-Blackness, appropriation, power dynamics, and more.[20] The more we each explore and become accountable to our role in these systems, the wider the circle of transformation becomes.

A broad coalition of humans of all races have always worked in solidarity to halt the impacts and decimate the structures of racial injustice. From Dolores Huerta[21] to Yuri Kochiyama,[22] to the Polynesian Panther Party,[23] humans en masse have aligned their energy and resources toward the goals of equity and justice. If you're committed to radical self-love as a social justice practice, you will need to do the same. Organizations like the Movement for Black Lives, United We Dream, Showing Up for Racial Justice (SURJ), Sister-Song, Indigenous People's Power Project, South Asian Americans Leading Together (SAALT), and Race Forward are plowing a road toward racial equity for their communities. Look them up, support them, join them. As Layla Saad says, let your efforts help you "become a good ancestor."

Battling All Body Terrorism

Get Willing to Risk

By no means is this chapter presented as a definitive manual for confronting body-based oppression. Issues of ageism, sexism, and oppressions that intersect with bodily identity like classism or xenophobia all persist and must be addressed, but this book would span the cosmos if I attempted to contain all these issues in these pages. No matter the problem we desire to solve, our work to eradicate all forms of body terrorism will overlap in several strategies. Excavating how we've absorbed and parroted the messages of body terrorism against specific bodies and groups of people will help us initiate new ways of thinking. It is this new thinking that urges us to uplift the lives of those outside the default, seeking out and elevating their histories, narratives, cultures, and experiences. By advocating for those in our sphere of influence to join us in expanding our knowledge and challenging our indoctrinated beliefs and ideas about those bodies, we engage new action or what we've called *doing*. And finally, when we join, support, and participate in the existing organized efforts to undo the manifestations of bodily hierarchy and amass our collective power, we destabilize the foundations of body terrorism, weaken its beams, and ultimately collapse its structures, leaving wide-open space to begin a new, loving way of being.

There are scholars, organizers, and activists who believe that interpersonal acts of body terrorism matter little to the larger experience of institutions and systems, proposing that the eradication of these systems is what will most impact the lives of marginalized people. Without question, the systemic manifestations of body terrorism have historically wrought the most significant long-term impacts of harm to those who are oppressed. However, as stated earlier, systems require our active or passive assistance to remain standing. And those consciously or subconsciously invested in and privileged by the system of bodily hierarchy will also have a vested interest in maintaining the present-day order of default bodies. Our individual and consolidated divestment from that system is what makes its continued existence untenable. But creating collective disruption in the system of body terrorism will require each of us to risk.

Change is impossible without risk. Those who live in bodies targeted most by body terrorism are forced to exist in a perpetual state of risk. Whether it be the risk of being misgendered when attempting to access services, like my nonbinary friend Emma, or being targeted for police state violence because of your race, mental health status, or both, like Kayla Moore,[24] or being denied employment or fair wages because of a developmental disability like my brother Daryl and sister Jozlynn. To live outside the default body is to be forced to balance upon a tightrope of constant social, political, economic, and bodily risk.

When our bodies are the default, we are asked to risk nearly nothing. We are given a refuge of social comfort in exchange for our compliance to a system of bodily hierarchy. Our barbecues and picnics go undisturbed, our family holiday dinners maintain a placid normalcy. We are afforded an existence of relative ease with those who share our default privilege while nondefault bodies absorb the compounding risks from which we've opted out. It is this version of comfort/complicity that we have come to prize over justice. What might become possible if each of us absorbed some of the risk placed on marginalized bodies? What if we refused to be accomplices to body terrorism in all its forms, personal and political?

There are small, everyday ways we are invited to interrupt our collusion with the comfort of body-based oppression in service of justice for all bodies. My opportunity to practice a small act of risk presented itself on a summer day in Aotearoa (New Zealand). A new neighbor, her husband, her friend, and I sat on their porch and watched the sun cast diamond flecks of light on the ocean's surface at Onetangi Beach on Waiheke Island, thirty miles off the coast of Auckland. We were engaged in simple, comfortable conversation when the topic veered in the direction of body shaming a friend who'd had by their estimation "lots" of plastic surgery. Before I could redirect the conversation away from body shame, one of the women threw out a completely unexpected transphobic comment.

This moment has presented itself a million times a day, in a million different settings, likely since the earliest points of history. Someone makes a comment steeped in the indoctrinations of body terrorism and those who do not agree are suddenly at a crossroad. Do we speak up or do we leave the moment and its default comfort intact? We ask ourselves, "Who am I to disrupt this pleasant day with my politics? What if they think I'm a troublemaker? What if I'm seen as not nice?" Each of us has been conditioned to collude with some form of body terrorism for the sake of preserving the default body's comfort. Consequently, we give way to continued oppression.

On that porch, I was given the opportunity to choose a budding act of justice over cisgender comfort. Choosing justice did not mean I had to detonate the afternoon with a self-righteous chastising of everyone within earshot. To the contrary, as a person with cisgender privilege it is my responsibility to hold with compassion the deep indoctrination of those with whom I share default status.

My (our) collective assignment is to challenge indoctrinations. There will be times when those challenges must be vociferous and aggressive. And there will be times when our choice to quietly but publicly disavow body terrorism will be the aperture needed to change hearts. On that small porch overlooking Onetangi Beach with a group of people I knew little about other than we shared a default identity of privilege, I made a small ripple in the myopic sphere of cis comfort. I said plainly, "I have some really amazing trans friends. They're incredibly powerful, beautiful, and important in the world. And that's who I know trans people to be." My porch companion stammered, apologized, and we moved on to why body shaming their friend was not going to help their friend love herself.

Each invitation to risk social comfort for an interpersonal act of justice disturbs the social contract of body terrorism. Even a small wrinkle in the bed of privilege is enough to force some of us awake. It is in our awakening that we accrue the collective power to bring into being a transformed world predicated on radical, unapologetic love.

Conclusion

Many summers ago, I sat on a hotel rooftop in Bahia, Brazil, with a gaggle of raucous and revolutionary Black feminist change makers. Over the course of three days, these women, who were flung there from every corner of the world, detonated my mind with their interminable brilliance and insight. They were unquestionably some of the most badass humans I had ever met. Sipping caipirinhas and cackling into the blue-black sky, my favorite rabble-rouser of the group, long-time activist and artist Kai (pronounced Ky-ee), in her half-teasing, wholly provocative way, queried the group, "We doing all this fighting for liberation. Any of y'all know what liberation looks like?"

Kai slapped the question down on the table like a dead fish, and the whole group was dumbstruck for a second. Quickly, answers began to stammer out of mouths like closing-time drunkards. It appeared many of us had never really given ourselves permission to ponder what a world rid of oppression might look like. My friends and comrades who were deeply involved in political movements from Ecuador to Houston, from farmworkers' rights to the Movement for Black Lives, wrestled with that small knot of a question well into the early morning hours. For many of us, the fight was so incessant, insisting on our every mental and emotional fiber for our survival, that rarely had we been given a moment to think about what might exist in our lives or on the planet when we finished fighting.

My answer was swift but silent. I said only to myself, "Radical self-love." Torn by what felt at once profoundly true and absurdly small, insignificant up against the global powers of oppression, I kept my answer inside. How could a concept so simple occupy the spaces that marginalization and separation had seemed to fill for centuries? But I knew that my follow-up question was a lie. My doubts were not about the efficacy of radical self-love. My doubts were about me. How dare I believe I have any answers for such complicated geopolitical and social quandaries? Who am I to even speak to these issues? How quickly the voice of self-doubt and deficiency ran in to fill the space in my head where radical self-love should have resided. My fear was not about what I didn't know. Example after example has apprised me of the same truth: the only thing that kills the slow, poisonous choke of body shame and body terrorism that dwells in each of us is radical self-love. That truth is not of me but through me, just like the first time I uttered the words "The body is not an apology." My work is simply to be a willing vessel for its message.

If I could go back to that night on a rooftop in Brazil and answer Kai's question, I would say, loudly and unapologetically, "Liberation is the opportunity for every human, no matter their body, to have unobstructed access to their highest self, for every human to live in radical self-love." I did not say it that night, but I am saying it now, to you, and I am not the least bit sorry.

Notes

Prologue

1. B. Brown, *Daring Greatly: How the Courage to Be Vulnerable Transforms the Way We Live, Love, Parent, and Lead* (London: Penguin, 2012), 69.

2. M. Williamson, "The Spiritual Purpose of Relationships" (lecture, Los Angeles, January 3, 2016).

Chapter 1

1. Adam Hayes, "Scalability," *Investopedia*, March 20, 2020, https://www.investopedia.com/terms/s/scalability.asp.

2. S. L. Cano, "Angela Davis to Speak March 4 at New York City Unity Rally," *People's World*, February 28, 2017, http://www.peoplesworld.org/article/angela-davis-to-speak-march-4-at-new-york-city-unity-rally.

3. L. S. Cahill and M. A. Farley, *Embodiment, Morality, and Medicine* (Dordrecht, the Netherlands: Kluwer Academic Publishers, 1995).

4. M. Moseley, "Ten Things to Know about the Heartbreaking Story of Kalief Browder," *Essence*, March 2, 2017, http://www.essence.com/news/facts-about-kalief-browder-rikers-prison-documentary-JayZ.

5. C. Eisenstein, *The More Beautiful World Our Hearts Know Is Possible* (Berkeley, CA: North Atlantic Books, 2013).

6. Maureen Benson is a general rock star and founder and CEO of the organization Education Is a Vital Sign.

7. Definition of *radical*, Dictionary.com, http://www.dictionary.com/browse/radical, accessed July 29, 2020.

8. N. Ghandnoosh, "Race and Punishment: Racial Perceptions of Crime and Support for Punitive Policies," The Sentencing Project, October 3, 2014, http://sentencingproject.org/wp-content/uploads/2015/11/Race-and-Punishment.pdf.

9. C. Liebowitz, "Explaining Inspiration Porn to Non-Disabled People," The Body Is Not an Apology, September 24, 2015, https://thebodyisnotanapology.com /magazine/explaining-inspiration-porn-to-non-disabled-people/.

10. "Africans in America," PBS, January 12, 2017, http://www.pbs.org/wgbh/aia /part2/2narr5.html.

11. "Voting Rights Act Timeline," ACLU, March 4, 2005, https://www.aclu.org /files/assets/voting_rights_act_timeline20111222.pdf.

12. Amend the Code for Marriage Equality Act of 2015, H.R. 2976, 114th Congress (2015–2016), July 8, 2015, https://www.congress.gov/bill/114th-congress /house-bill/2976.

13. D. Masci, E. Scuipac, and M. Lipka, *Gay Marriage around the World*, Pew Research Center's Religion and Public Life Project, October 28, 2019, https:// www.pewforum.org/fact-sheet/gay-marriage-around-the-world/.

14. C. Domonoske and J. Doubek, "North Carolina Repeals Portions of Controversial 'Bathroom Bill,'" NPR, March 30, 2017, http://www.npr.org/sections /thetwo-way/2017/03/30/522009335/north-carolina-lawmakers-governor -announce-compromise-to-repeal-bathroom-bill.

15. "Persons with a Disability: Labor Force Characteristics," Bureau of Labor Statistics, June 21, 2016, https://www.bls.gov/news.release/disabl.htm.

16. K. Crenshaw, "Mapping the Margins: Intersectionality, Identity Politics, and Violence against Women of Color," *Stanford Law Review* 43, no. 6 (1991): 1241, doi:10.2307/1229039.

17. Hanne Blank, "Hanne Blank's Real Women," Behind Body Peace, July 18, 2011, bodypeaceblog.wordpress.com/2011/07/18/hanne-blanks-real-women/.

18. D. B. Taylor, "Mama Cax, Amputee Model and Disability Activist, Dies at 30," *New York Times*, December 22, 2019, https://www.nytimes.com/2019/12/22 /fashion/Mama-cax-dead.html.

19. J. Gallagher, "'Memories' Pass between Generations," BBC, December 1, 2013, http://www.bbc.com/news/health-25156510.

20. "The Death of Emmett Till," History.com, http://www.history.com/this-day-in -history/the-death-of-emmett-till, accessed July 29, 2020.

21. J. Sauers, "French *Elle*'s First 'Curvy' Issue Introduces Us to Tara Lynn, Capes," *Jezebel*, March 30, 2010, https://jezebel.com/5505614/french-elles-first-curvy -issue-introduces-us-to-tara-lynn-capes/.

22. S. Taylor, "Mission, Vision, and History," The Body Is Not an Apology, https:// thebodyisnotanapology.com/about-tbinaa/history-mission-and-vision/, accessed July 29, 2020.

23. "Acceptance vs. Resignation," *Secular Buddhism*, February 24, 2016, https://secularbuddhism.com/acceptance-vs-resignation/.

24. T. R. Echeverria, "Audre Lorde: A Black, Lesbian, Mother, Socialist, Warrior, Poet," Solidarity, February 18, 2012, https://www.solidarity-us.org/site/node/3525.

25. Health at Every Size supports people of all sizes in addressing their health directly by encouraging the adoption of healthy behaviors. It is an inclusive movement, recognizing that our social characteristics, such as our size, race, national origin, sexuality, gender, disability status, and other attributes, are assets. It acknowledges and challenges the structural and systemic forces that impinge on living well. See https://haescommunity.com/.

26. D. Burgard, "The Problem with Poodle Science," YouTube video, February 23, 2015, https://www.youtube.com/watch?v=H89QQfXtc-k.

27. Sabrina Strings, *Fearing the Black Body: The Racial Origins of Fatphobia* (New York: New York University Press, 2019).

28. "You are in the right place" is a common greeting for newcomers to twelve-step meetings.

Chapter 2

1. R. Bender, "The Age Girls Become Self-Conscious about Their Bodies," *Yahoo! News,* January 12, 2016, https://www.yahoo.com/news/the-age-girls-become-self-1338923817869366.html.

2. "Webinars and Online Courses," The Body Is Not an Apology, https://thebodyisnotanapology.com/radical-education/webinars/, accessed July 29, 2020.

3. For preferred terminology, refer to the website Gender Diversity, "Elementary Schools," Gender Diversity, November 6, 2017, www.genderdiversity.org/best-practices-schools/elementary/.

4. A. H. Grossman and A. R. D'Augelli, "Transgender Youth and Life-Threatening Behaviors," *Suicide and Life-Threatening Behavior* 37, no. 5 (2007): 527–537, http://onlinelibrary.wiley.com/doi/10.1521/suli.2007.37.5.527/abstract.

5. M. B. Brewer, "In-Group Bias in the Minimal Intergroup Situation: A Cognitive-Motivational Analysis," *Psychological Bulletin* 86, no. 2 (1979): 307–324, http://psycnet.apa.org/psycinfo/1979-25967-001.

6. "DBR MTV Bias Survey Summary," April 2014, p. 3, https://www.evernote.com/shard/s4/sh/5edc56c3-f8c8-483f-a459-2c47192d0bb8/a0ba0ce883749f4e613d6a6338bb4455/res/5cff2161-7c98-4c9a-9830-a900c7496644/DBR_MTV_Bias_Survey_Executive_Summary.pdf.

7. "Children, Teens, Media, and Body Image: A Common Sense Media Research Brief," Children, Teens, Media, and Body Image, Common Sense Media, January 21, 2015, www.commonsensemedia.org/research/children-teens-media-and-body-image.

8. S. Sumapong, "Toxic Masculinity and the Negative Effects on Men," Good Men Project, November 18, 2016, https://goodmenproject.com/featured-content/toxic-masculinity-and-the-negative-effects-on-men-babb/.

9. C. Knorr, "Boys and Body Image," Common Sense Media, January 5, 2015, https://www.commonsensemedia.org/blog/boys-and-body-image#.

10. bell hooks, *All about Love* (New York: Harper Perennial, 2000).

11. Adrienne M. Brown, *Pleasure Activism: The Politics of Feeling Good* (Chico, CA: AK Press, 2019).

12. J. Bakutyte, "A Look at the History of Women's Beauty," *A Plus*, November 5, 2014, http://aplus.com/a/history-female-beauty-standards/.

13. K. Gaylor, "A Royal Queer: Hatshepsut and Gender Construction in Ancient Egypt," *Shift Journal* 8 (2015): 1–11, http://shiftjournal.org/wp-content/uploads/2015/11/4_Gaylord.pdf.

14. "Timeline: Transgender through History," *Doc Zone*, CBC/Radio Canada, April 10, 2013, http://www.cbc.ca/doczone/features/timeline-transgender-through-history.

15. D. R. Roediger, *Working toward Whiteness: How America's Immigrants Became White: The Strange Journey from Ellis Island to the Suburbs* (New York: Basic Books, 2010).

16. "Ad Age Advertising Century: Timeline," *Ad Age*, March 29, 1999, http://adage.com/article/special-report-the-advertising-century/ad-age-advertising-century-timeline/143661/.

17. A. Guttmann, "Global Advertising Spending 2019," Statista, January 8, 2020, www.statista.com/statistics/236943/global-advertising-spending/.

18. Bethany Biron, "Beauty Has Blown Up to Be a $532 Billion Industry—and Analysts Say That These 4 Trends Will Make It Even Bigger," Business Insider, July 9, 2019, www.businessinsider.com/beauty-multibillion-industry-trends-future-2019-7.

19. "World Economic Outlook Database October 2019," International Monetary Fund, October 2019, www.imf.org/external/pubs/ft/weo/2019/02/weodata/weorept.aspx?pr.x=64 . . .

20. "Self-Image and Media Influence," Just Say Yes, February 28, 2017, https://www.justsayyes.org/topics/self-image-media-influences/.

21. Alexis Bennett, "Women Spend on Average $15,000 on Beauty Products— Here's Proof," SELF, May 25, 2017, www.self.com/story/amount-of-money -women-spend-on-beauty-products.

22. "Hot, in style, popular, 'damn, that song was poppin' back in the day,'" definition of *poppin'*, Urban Dictionary, https://www.urbandictionary.com/define .php?term=poppin, accessed July 29, 2020.

23. G. Beemyn, "Transgender Terminology," Cornell.edu, April 27, 2017, https://hr.cornell.edu/sites/default/files/trans%20terms.pdf.

24. "Map of Countries That Criminalise LGBT People," Human Dignity Trust, www.humandignitytrust.org/lgbt-the-law/map-of-criminalisation/, accessed August 14, 2020.

25. "Health Requirements," New Zealand Immigration Concepts, https://www .new-zealand-immigration.com/, accessed July 29, 2020.

26. Susan M. Schweik and Robert A. Wilson, "Ugly Laws," Eugenics Archives, February 5, 2015, https://eugenicsarchive.ca/discover/tree/54d39e27f8a0ea4706000009.

27. H. Schwarz, "Following Reports of Forced Sterilization of Female Prison Inmates, California Passes Ban," *Washington Post,* September 26, 2014, https:// www.washingtonpost.com/blogs/govbeat/wp/2014/09/26/following-reports -of-forced-sterilization-of-female-prison-inmates-california-passes-ban/.

28. A. N. Ltd, "With This Ring, I Thee Abduct," *Times of Malta,* February 25, 2015, http://www.timesofmalta.com/articles/view/20150225/local/with-this-ring-i -thee-abduct.557594.

29. D. Artavia, "Greece Reinstates Forced HIV Testing," *Plus,* July 22, 2013, http://www.hivplusmag.com/case-studies/world-news/2013/07/22/greece -reinstates-forced-hiv-testing.

30. "History of Women Governors," Center for American Women in Politics, http://www.cawp.rutgers.edu/history-women-governors, accessed July 29, 2020.

31. "Fast Facts about American Governors," Rutgers University, February 27, 2017, http://governors.rutgers.edu/on-governors/us-governors/fast-facts-about -american-governors/.

32. "Female World Leaders Currently in Power," World Bank, http://data .worldbank.org/indicator/SG.GEN.PARL.ZS, accessed July 29, 2020.

33. N. Wolf, *The Beauty Myth: How Images of Beauty Are Used against Women* (New York: Harper Perennial, 2002), 187.

34. "List of Minority Governors and Lieutenant Governors in the United States," Wikipedia, Wikimedia Foundation, July 31, 2020, en.wikipedia.org/wiki/List_of _minority_governors_and_lieutenant_governors_in_the_United_States.

35. I. Langtree, "List of Physically Disabled World Leaders and Politicians," Disabled-World.com, July 29, 2015, https://www.disabled-world.com/disability /awareness/famous/leaders-pollies.php.

36. C. Domonoske, "For First Time, Openly LGBTQIAA+ Governor Elected: Oregon's Kate Brown," NPR, November 9, 2016, http://www.npr.org/sections /thetwo-way/2016/11/09/501338927/for-first-time-openly-LGBTQIAA+ -gove rnor-elected-oregons-kate-brown.

37. S. Tavernise, "U.S. Suicide Rate Surges to a 30-Year High," *New York Times*, April 22, 2016, https://www.nytimes.com/2016/04/22/health/us-suicide-rate -surges-to-a-30-year-high.html.

38. R. Gabrielson, R. Grochowski Jones, and E. Sagara, "Deadly Force, in Black and White," ProPublica, December 24, 2014, https://www.propublica.org/article /deadly-force-in-black-and-white.

39. "More Than 115 Anti-LGBTQIAA+ Bills Introduced in 30 States," Human Rights Campaign, March 22, 2017, https://www.hrc.org/blog/more-than-115 -anti-LGBTQIAA+ -bills-introduced-in-30-states/.

40. F. Fox, "Leelah Alcorn's Suicide: Conversion Therapy Is Child Abuse," *Time*, January 8, 2015, http://time.com/3655718/leelah-alcorn-suicide-transgender -therapy.

41. Definition of *terrorism*, Merriam-Webster.com, https://www.merriam-webster .com/dictionary/terrorism/, accessed July 29, 2020.

42. "What Is Body Terrorism?" The Body Is Not an Apology, accessed January 29, 2017, https://thebodyisnotanapology.com/about-tbinaa/what-is-body-terrorism/, accessed July 29, 2020.

Chapter 3

1. From the website of Davide Carrera, accessed April 23, 2017, http://www.david ecarrera.com/.

2. "Arabs as Terrorists: The Power of Media Images," Society of Personality and Social Psychology, December 9, 2012, https://spsptalks.wordpress.com/2012/12 /07/arabs-as-terrorists-the-power-of-media-images.

3. A. Willingham, "Chances of a Refugee Killing You—and Other Surprising Immigration Stats," CNN.com, March 6, 2017, http://www.cnn.com/2017/01/30 /politics/immigration-stats-by-the-numbers-trnd/.

4. J. E. Short, "How Much Media?" Business.tivo.com, October 2013, https:// business.tivo.com/content/dam/tivo/resources/tivo-HMM-Consumer-Report -2013_Release.pdf.

5. E. Ensler, "Suddenly My Body," TED video, December 2011, https://www.ted.com/talks/eve_ensler_suddenly_my_body.

6. N. Waheed, "Three," Words for the Year, June 1, 2015, https://wordsfortheyear.com/2015/06/04/three-by-nayyirah-waheed/.

7. A. C. Liebowitz, "Here's What Neurodiversity Is—And What It Means for Feminism," Everyday Feminism, March 3, 2016, http://everydayfeminism.com/2016/03/neurodiversity-101/.

Chapter 4

1. "Understanding Implicit Bias," Kirwan Institute for the Study of Race and Ethnicity, 2015, http://kirwaninstitute.osu.edu/research/understanding-implicit-bias/.

2. L. Watson, Lilla: International Women's Network, January 27, 2010, https://lillanetwork.wordpress.com/about/.

3. G. L. Boggs, *Living for Change: An Autobiography* (Minneapolis: University of Minnesota Press, 2016), 146.

4. *Slavery by Another Name* (documentary), directed by Samuel D. Pollard, aired on PBS, February 13, 2012, http://www.pbs.org/tpt/slavery-by-another-name/themes/convict-leasing/.

5. "Black Codes," History.com, 2010, http://www.history.com/topics/black-history/black-codes.

6. M. Alexander, *The New Jim Crow* (New York: New Press, 2012), 2.

7. "Six Other Times the US Has Banned Immigrants," *Al Jazeera*, January 29, 2017, http://www.aljazeera.com/indepth/features/2017/01/times-banned-immigrants-170128183528941.html.

8. "Immigration," Center for HIV Law and Policy, https://www.hivlawandpolicy.org/issues/immigration, accessed July 29, 2020.

9. D. Merica, "Hillary Clinton Speaks with Black Lives Matter Activists," CNN, August 18, 2015, http://www.cnn.com/2015/08/18/politics/hillary-clinton-black-lives-matter-meeting/.

10. "Hillary Clinton: Equality Is about Changing Hearts and Minds," YouTube video, October 21, 2016, https://www.youtube.com/watch?v=kuxdbBPSnas.

11. Washington Governor Jay Inslee, "Inslee Statement in Response to Washingtonians Detained at Canadian Border," January 6, 2020, https://www.governor.wa.gov/news-media/inslee-statement-response-washingtonians-detained-canadian-border.

12. M. Inman, "You're Not Going to Believe What I Am about to Tell You," The Oatmeal, July 23, 2017, http://theoatmeal.com/comics/believe.

13. J. L. Anderson, *Che Guevara: A Revolutionary Life* (New York: Grove Press, 2010), 178.

14. Alcoholics Anonymous, "A.A. Big Book Promises," https://step12.com /promises.html.

Chapter 5

1. A. Brown, *Emergent Strategy: Shaping Change, Changing World* (Chico, CA: AK Press, 2017).

2. L. Piepzna-Samarasinha, *Care Work: Dreaming Disability Justice* (Vancouver, BC: Arsenal Pulp, 2018), 78.

3. R. Puhl, S. Phelan, J. Nadglowski, and T. Kyle, "Overcoming Weight Bias in the Management of Patients with Diabetes and Obesity," *Clinical Diabetes* 34, no. 1 (2016): 44–50, https://pubmed.ncbi.nlm.nih.gov/26807008/.

4. Original Intuitive Eating Pros, "10 Principles of Intuitive Eating," https://www .intuitiveeating.org/10-principles-of-intuitive-eating/, accessed July 29, 2020.

5. Health at Every Size Community Resources, https://haescommunity.com/, accessed July 29, 2020.

6. Sabrina Strings, *Fearing the Black Body: The Racial Origins of Fatphobia* (New York: New York University Press, 2019).

7. Association for Size Diversity and Health, https://www.sizediversityandhealth .org/, accessed July 29, 2020.

8. NOLOSE: The Revolution Just Got Bigger, https://nolose.org/, accessed July 29, 2020.

9. Sins Invalid, https://www.sinsinvalid.org/.

10. "10 Principles of Disability Justice," Sins Invalid, September 17, 2015, https:// www.sinsinvalid.org/blog/10-principles-of-disability-justice.

11. "Queer Like, Escaping Definition," Decolonize the Queer, https://decolonizet hequeer.wordpress.com/2015/01/15/queer-like-escaping-definition/.

12. Visual artist and founder of Culture Strike Favianna Rodriguez was the first person I heard using the term *compost* to describe transforming unhealthy systems and behaviors into fuel for a new way of being. Check her out at https://www .favianna.com/.

13. Walter J. Williams, "The 'Two-Spirit' People of Indigenous North Americans," *Guardian*, October 11, 2010, https://www.theguardian.com/music/2010/oct/11 /two-spirit-people-north-america.

14. History, "Stonewall Riots," June 26, 2020, https://www.history.com/topics /gay-rights/the-stonewall-riots.

15. "Transgender Day of Remembrance," GLAAD, https://www.glaad.org/tdor.

16. Diffen, "Equality vs. Equity," https://www.diffen.com/difference/Equality-vs
-Equity, accessed July 29, 2020.

17. Ijeoma Oluo, *So You Want to Talk about Race* (Berkeley, CA: Seal Press, 2018).

18. "Seeing White," Scene on Radio, 2020, https://www.sceneonradio.org/seeing
-white/.

19. Robin DiAngelo, *White Fragility: Why It's So Hard for White People to Talk
about Racism* (Boston: Beacon Press, 2018).

20. Layla F. Saad, *Me and White Supremacy* (Naperville, IL: Sourcebooks, 2020).

21. Dolores Huerta Foundation, https://doloreshuerta.org/dolores-huerta/.

22. "Yuri Kochiyama," Wonder Women, https://www.wndrwmn.com/yuri
-kochiyama.

23. Polynesian Panthers Party, https://polynesianpanthersparty.weebly.com
/polynesian-panthers.html.

24. Berkeley Copwatch, "Justice 4 Kayla Moore," https://www.berkeleycopwatch
.org/justice-for-kayla-moore, accessed July 29, 2020.

Radical Resources

The only way to fight an entire world built on body shame is to build a world of radical self-love around ourselves. Leaving the land of body shame can feel like the world's loneliest exile, but it need not be. There are thousands of activists, organizations, and media sources doing work to create a just world for our different bodies. Below I've listed only a few. Visit these websites to learn more.

Radical Self-Love
The Body Is Not an Apology   https://thebodyisnotanapology.com/

Weight Stigma Resources
Nalgona Positivity Pride   https://www.nalgonapositivitypride.com/
Association for Size Diversity and Health (ASDAH)
        https://www.sizediversityandhealth.org/
National Association to Advance Fat Acceptance (NAAFA)
        https://naafa.org/
NOLOSE   http://nolose.org/
Health at Every Size   https://haescommunity.com/

Racial Justice Resources
The Movement for Black Lives   https://m4bl.org/
Race Forward   https://www.raceforward.org/
Black Youth Project 100   http://byp100.org/
Showing Up for Racial Justice   https://www.showingupforracialjustice.org/
United We Dream   https://unitedwedream.org/

Disability Justice Resources

Disability Justice   http://disabilityjustice.org/

Sins Invalid   http://www.sinsinvalid.org/

Leah Lakshmi Piepzna-Samarasinha   http://www.brownstargirl.org/

ADAPT   http://adapt.org/

Fireweed Collective   https://fireweedcollective.org/

LGBTQIAA+ Resources

Transgender Law Center (TLC)   https://transgenderlawcenter.org/

GLAAD   https://www.glaad.org/

Southerners on New Ground   http://southernersonnewground.org/

Astrea Foundation   https://www.astraeafoundation.org/

Trans Lifeline   https://www.translifeline.org/ US: (877) 565-8860

Canada: (877) 330-6366

Aging Resources

National Council on Aging   https://www.ncoa.org/

Advocacy and Services for LGBTQIAA+ Elders

https://www.sageusa.org/

National Asian Pacific Center on Aging   http://napca.org/

HelpAge USA   https://www.helpageusa.org/

Acknowledgments

Since the first edition of this book was released, both my internal world and our collective world have changed in ways I was simply incapable of imagining back then. We have learned the intricacies of how a virus can spread around the world. We have watched the ceaseless machine of body terrorism crush lives before our very eyes on phones and laptops. And we have witnessed what the world looks like when we collectively say NO MORE and begin to slowly turn toward radical self-love. During this slingshot of massive social change, I have been blessed to be held sweetly and quietly by the whenua of Aotearoa and the love of the tangata whenua (people of the land) Māori. I want to mihi to the rich indomitable spirit of the Indigenous people of New Zealand who welcomed me and allowed me to heal in their home.

Specifically, I want to thank Kiterangi Cameron, the Cameron family, and their Māori family liberation organization, Tu Tama Wahine o Taranaki. I was so beautifully adopted into their whanau and guided with deep love, and it was through their generosity that I began to rediscover and understand my own indigeneity. I am forever grateful and on the side of Māori liberation and justice. Tino rangatiratanga! Thank you, Glen Bennet, for housing me as I completed this project and prepared for the next wild adventure. Thank you, Shannon Weber, for singularly holding the digital face of TBINAA while I did whatever the hell I was doing! You are a champion and a master conveyor of the spirit of this work.

I want to thank Emma Walter for being an essential partner of care and love in my evolution and a soul I will always love. Your care made so much possible. I want to thank my ancestors and divine guides who knew there was work in me to be done to bring forth the truest manifestation of this vision of radical self-love. They knew I had to learn to practice it in the most intimate and innermost ways, and BOY, did they give me exceptional opportunities to do so. I am gobsmacked by how much they love me. Grandma, Mommy, and Patoot, thank you for clearing the path and walking beside me. Thank you for knowing beyond what I know and holding me gently into Being. I am, indeed, chosen.

If you are reading this, keep going. We're almost there.

Index

ableism: body-based oppression and, 24; body terrorism and, 88; default body and, 37; LGBTQIAA+ bodies and, 60; origins of, 5, 84–85; strategies for fighting against, 111–115. *See also* disabilities (diasbled bodies)

abuse: body shame and, 40; self-abuse, 40, 80; sexual abuse, 40

acceptance, x; *vs.* compliance, 22–23; of discomfort, while practicing radical self-love, 95; self-acceptance, 3–4, 6–7; as tool for expansion, 22

acquiescence, 3–4

addiction, 60, 79

adults: body-shame consciousness survey, 31; consequences of body terrorism, 85; media consumption data, 72; minimizing of "different" by, 37; perceptions of love by, 40; shaming of children by, 37; shaming of teens, 32–33

advertising: global spending data (2018), 44–45; portrayal of the female body, 45–46; role in creating body shame, 73–74; television industry income data, 74. *See also* media

African chattel slave trade, 25

ageism, 5, 60, 88, 124

agender people, 118

Alcorn, Leelah, 57

Alexander, Michelle, 90–91

All About Love (hooks), 40

anorexia nervosa, 60

anti-immigrant activism, U.S., 91–93

AOL.com survey (2014), 38

apologies/apologizing: dismantling the culture of, 15–19; feeling discouraged and, 17; female Black bodies and, 12–13; reasons for, 14–15; self-evaluation and, 17–18; unapologetic power and, 18–19. *See also* Unapologetic Inquiries

Aristotle, 5

Asexualization Act (1909), California, 52

asexual people, 118

Asian model-minority myth, 122

Association for Size Diversity and Health (ASDAH), 110

authenticity: taking risks for, x

Beauty Myth, The (Wolf), 53

"being" strategy: for fighting against ableism, 113–115; for fighting against fatphobia, 109–111; for fighting against queerism and transphobia, 118; for fighting against racial inequity, 122–123

Benson, Maureen, 6

About the Author

Sonya Renee Taylor *is a world-renowned activist, author, artist, spiritual, transformational leader, and the founder of The Body Is Not an Apology, a movement and digital media and education company exploring the intersections of identity, healing, and social justice using the framework of radical self-love. The Body Is Not An Apology's content and message have changed the lives of millions of people across the globe, shifting how we live in and relate to our bodies and the bodies of others, shifting from a relationship of shame and injustice to a relationship bound by love. She is the author of six books, including* Celebrate Your Body (and Its Changes, Too!), The Book of Radical Answers (That I Know You Already Know) *(Dial Press 2022) and coeditor of* The International Handbook of Fat Studies *(Routledge 2021). Her writing appears in numerous anthologies and magazines. Sonya is an international-award-winning performance poet and speaker who has appeared across the United States, New Zealand, Australia, England, Scotland, Sweden, Germany, Brazil, Canada, the Netherlands, Bosnia, and more. Sonya and her work have appeared on CBS, CNN, NPR, HBO, BET, MTV, TV One, PBS, MSNBC.com, Today.com, Shape.com, and in the* New York Times, New York *magazine,* Huffington Post, Vogue Australia, Playboy, Self, Ms. *magazine, and many more*

forums. Sonya was a 2016 invitee to the Obama White House to speak on the intersection of LGBTQIAA+ and disability issues. In 2017, she was an inaugural selectee of the Edmund Hillary Fellowship for global impact change makers. Sonya has shared the stage with such luminaries as Angela Davis, Sonia Sanchez, Amy Goodman, Carrie Mae Weems, Theaster Gates, Harry Belafonte, Dr. Cornel West, Hillary Rodham Clinton, the late Amiri Baraka, and numerous others. She continues to perform, teach, and transform lives globally. Visit her at www.sonya reneetaylor.com.

About TBINAA

The Body Is Not an Apology is a digital media and education company committed to cultivating global radical self-love and body empowerment as the foundational tool for social justice and global transformation. We believe that discrimination, social inequality, and injustice are manifestations of our inability to make peace with the body, our own and others'. Utilizing the power of technology, media, education, and community building, The Body Is Not an Apology fosters global, radical, unapologetic self-love, which translates to radical human love and action in service toward a more just, equitable, and compassionate world. Join the hundreds of thousands of people who are reading radical self-love articles and content at www.TheBodyIsNotAnApology.com.

Also by Sonya Renee Taylor

Your Body Is Not an Apology Worbook

Tools for Living Radical Self-Love

Readers of *The Body Is Not an Apology* have been clamoring for guidance on how to do the work of radical self-love. After crowd-sourcing in her community, Sonya Renee Taylor found her readers wanted more concrete ideas on how to apply this work to their daily lives. *Your Body Is Not an Apology Workbook* is the action guide that gives them just that—tools and structured frameworks they can apply immediately to start changing their lives. Taylor guides readers with concrete ideas and, as always, practical appli-cations that move us beyond theory and into doing and being radi-cal self-love change agents in our own lives and in the world. This workbook, along with the new edition of the book, will put people in action in their homes, families, doctor's offices, and jobs.

Available April 6, 2021
Paperback, ISBN 978-1-5230-9116-4
PDF ebook, ISBN 978-1-5230-9117-1
ePub ebook, ISBN 978-1-5230-9118-8

BK Berrett–Koehler Publishers, Inc.
www.bkconnection.com   **800.929.2929**

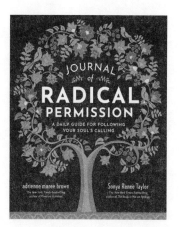

Journal of Radical Permission

The Journal of Radical Permission provides a beautiful experience of journaling your way toward your most authentic self. It helps readers uproot old patterns and make unconditional self-acceptance a reality. While the journal can be used on its own as part of your healing journey, it's based on the Institute for Radical Permission and is best used as a companion to the course.

Journaling to these prompts will help you surrender to your body's needs instead of forcing yourself into cramped disciplines. It will encourage you to become awed by the natural beauty of your divine self instead of being rampantly self-critical. It will aid you in embracing your shadows and accepting responsibility for your impact all while liberating you to just be.

This structured journal provides six key practices, with prompts for each practice that center on curiosity, surrender, grace, and satisfaction. The daily prompts for self-inquiry can be used as part of your transformative journey.

Paperback, ISBN 978-1-5230-0242-9
PDF ebook, ISBN 978-1-5230-0243-6
ePub ebook, ISBN 978-1-5230-0244-3

BK Berrett–Koehler Publishers, Inc.
www.bkconnection.com

Berrett–Koehler
Publishers

Berrett-Koehler is an independent publisher dedicated to an ambitious mission: *Connecting people and ideas to create a world that works for all.*

Our publications span many formats, including print, digital, audio, and video. We also offer online resources, training, and gatherings. And we will continue expanding our products and services to advance our mission.

We believe that the solutions to the world's problems will come from all of us, working at all levels: in our society, in our organizations, and in our own lives. Our publications and resources offer pathways to creating a more just, equitable, and sustainable society. They help people make their organizations more humane, democratic, diverse, and effective (and we don't think there's any contradiction there). And they guide people in creating positive change in their own lives and aligning their personal practices with their aspirations for a better world.

And we strive to practice what we preach through what we call "The BK Way." At the core of this approach is *stewardship,* a deep sense of responsibility to administer the company for the benefit of all of our stakeholder groups, including authors, customers, employees, investors, service providers, sales partners, and the communities and environment around us. Everything we do is built around stewardship and our other core values of *quality, partnership, inclusion,* and *sustainability.*

This is why Berrett-Koehler is the first book publishing company to be both a B Corporation (a rigorous certification) and a benefit corporation (a for-profit legal status), which together require us to adhere to the highest standards for corporate, social, and environmental performance. And it is why we have instituted many pioneering practices (which you can learn about at www.bkconnection.com), including the Berrett-Koehler Constitution, the Bill of Rights and Responsibilities for BK Authors, and our unique Author Days.

We are grateful to our readers, authors, and other friends who are supporting our mission. We ask you to share with us examples of how BK publications and resources are making a difference in your lives, organizations, and communities at www.bkconnection.com/impact.

Dear reader,

Thank you for picking up this book and welcome to the worldwide BK community! You're joining a special group of people who have come together to create positive change in their lives, organizations, and communities.

What's BK all about?

Our mission is to connect people and ideas to create a world that works for all.

Why? Our communities, organizations, and lives get bogged down by old paradigms of self-interest, exclusion, hierarchy, and privilege. But we believe that can change. That's why we seek the leading experts on these challenges—and share their actionable ideas with you.

A welcome gift

To help you get started, we'd like to offer you a **free copy** of one of our bestselling ebooks:

www.bkconnection.com/welcome

When you claim your **free ebook**, you'll also be subscribed to our blog.

Our freshest insights

Access the best new tools and ideas for leaders at all levels on our blog at ideas.bkconnection.com.

Sincerely,

Your friends at Berrett-Koehler

Certified

Corporation